Praise for Tales from a Mountain Town

"Sharing both the lighthearted and intense aspects
of mountain town life, Buchanan delivers a vivid
glimpse of the inspired—and inspirational—
communities that define Colorado's high country.
     —Jason Blevins, The Denver Post

Eugene is a fantastic athlete and a gifted storyteller who's
spent most of his life living in mountain towns. Which makes
his personal anecdotes and character profiles that much more
authentic and fun to read. Eugene's writing will make you want
to pick up and move to the mountains after the first chapter."
     —Joe Carberry, Senior Editor, The Inertia

"Buchanan is the role model for anyone who has ever dreamed
of living the authentic mountain town life. A fun and easy-
to-read road map for anyone dreaming of doing the same."
     —Doug Schnitzpahn,
     Editor, Elevation Outdoors

TALES
FROM A
MOUNTAIN
TOWN

Musings From 25 Years of
Living in the Colorado Rockies

Eugene Buchanan

Library of Congress Cataloging-in-Publication Data

Buchanan, Eugene
    Tales from a Mountain Town / Eugene Buchanan. p. cm.

ISBN #: 978-0-692-99212-8

Printed in the United States of America by
IngramSpark (www.ingramspark.com)

Cover/interior design: Veronika Khanisenko
Illustrations: Mack Maschmeier

Recreation Publishing Inc.
P.O. Box 775589
Steamboat Springs, CO 80477;
 (970) 870-1376/(970) 846-6581
For individual copies visit www.eugenebuchanan.com

Retailers, please order through Ingram Book Group
(www.ingramspark.com)

First Edition

14 13 12 11 10 / 10 9 8 7 6 5 4 3 2 1

Foreword

It struck me, when standing with fly rod in the middle of the Yampa River, what this book is all about. Dangling through my wader belt was a lacrosse stick, and a snowbrush with trampoline netting attached. It was 6 p.m. in late October, and we had just returned from a youth hockey tournament in the Front Range. After driving through a maze of lions and ladybugs trick-or-treating our neighborhood, I was eager for some fresh air so I headed out fishing. The only problem: my net was in our other car. So I improvised.

With daylight waning, I fastened our tramp's net pocket, which I had recently taken down for the winter, to a snowbrush, and used a spare bike spoke to spread the opening. Rudimentary, sure, and not likely to appear in a Sage catalog, but hopefully effective. As I was leaving, my eyes landed on my lacrosse stick by the stairs. Maybe that would work better? So I brought both.

While I'm likely the only person ever to have fished with such contraptions, it hit me mid-cast: These are the kinds of situations I've often found myself in in 25 years of living in the Colorado mountain town of Steamboat Springs. And that's the genre of story you'll find inside these pages. Many of these stories have appeared elsewhere—in such periodicals as Powder, Skiing, Paddler, Canoe & Kayak, Outside, Elevation Outdoors, Steamboat Living and Steamboat Today—and I'd like to thank those publications for putting up with my antics. And I'd like to thank you for embracing my effort to put them in a book.

That was certainly easier, anyway, than putting fish in my homemade nets. Truth be told, I didn't get to see how either contraption would fare; my lone catch threw the hook before they could bear fruit, if not fish. Which is probably a good thing. The lacrosse pocket was likely a hair small and taught, and the tramp netting a tad deep. Hopefully, there's a story inside these pages that fits your tastes better.

— Eugene Buchanan

For my daughters, Brooke and Casey;
may you grow to tell your own tales
from a mountain town as well.

Other books by Eugene Buchanan:

Brothers on the Bashkaus
Comrades on the Colca
Outdoor Parents Outdoor Kids
Ultimate Canoe & Kayak Adventures

www.eugenebuchanan.com

Special thanks to the following Tales from a Mountain Town Sponsors:

Table of Contents

S • N • O • W

Table of Contents

W • A • T • E • R

L • A • N • D

Table of Contents

A • I • R
(All Interest/Random)

S • N • O • W

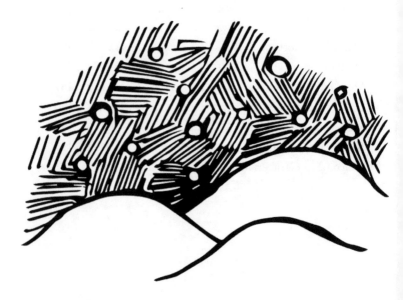

117 Guest Days and Counting

A lot of people have grandiose dreams of building a house in a ski town. A minimal commute to the slopes, a ski rack inside the front door, a crackling fire...maybe even a strategically positioned "dump" light outside the living room that lets you monitor snowfall.

But after we built our home in the Fairview neighborhood of town, we learned it's not without its pitfalls. It's not the property taxes or snowplow bills that cause consternation, but the guests and their License to Poach floorspace. It doesn't matter if they're invited or not: they all take up the same amount of room, use the same amount of toilet paper and leave the same number of socks buried in the sofa.

At first it didn't bother us: My wife and I were excited to show our 1,800 square feet of log-strewn splendor to less fortunate souls from the city. Besides, I had more than a few favors to repay from my time spent on the other end of the couch.

We didn't start keeping track of the accommodation avalanche until it began to rumble out of control. Trash cans overflowed, the coffee maker sounded its last gurgle and ground pads lay scattered in a half-curled disarray. The municipality also began to take notice: bottles flowed incessantly to the recycle curb; our electric meter spun like a compass at the North Pole; and the sanitation department called in for reinforcements.

The motel mayhem started Thanksgiving weekend when Tim showed up with three friends. Counting each body imprint as one "guest night" (four people, two nights), the tally quickly soared to eight. Two days later Jeff, an old highschool friend, arrived, staying for six nights and bringing the total to 14. Then came the in-laws...cousins from Nebraska outfitted with 160-cm. skis with safety straps and silver-toed Tyrolias. Three of them for two nights, snowballing the count to 20 before the holiday season even started. A few stragglers brought us to Christmas and the dreaded Family Onslaught. Mom, sister, sister's husband, another sister, brother, another brother, brother's wife. Three nights each, except for mom who stayed four more until she could completely rearrange the kitchen. The day she left saw the couch pillows fluffed just in time for John and Keith, more holdouts from high school: two more nights, bringing the total to 49. Then it was my wife's turn to contribute to the count as her twin, overlapping with John and Keith, set up camp for nine nights. Fifty-eight and counting.

A brief reprieve let us vacuum and restock paper towels before the next deluge. By February's Winter Carnival weekend, two more sets of friends had played weekend warrior, and a brother and repeat visitor had returned for seconds. Then came the Great Infiltration, six friends for two nights, followed by the Second Coming of Mom and the Father- and Mother-in-law Penetration. Eighty-nine and it was only mid-February. Things slowed down, but we eclipsed the 100 milestone on March 19 with another visit from Thanksgiving Tim. The Infant Infringement, consisting of two couples, two cribs and two food-flinging babies, brought the total to 112 (we had no problem treating the babies as equals in the tally). By season's end, the final number would read 117, with dogs adding another 32.

The folks at Guinness might not have a couch-surfer record in their annual compilation—and if they did, it'd likely be behind egg-eating and pogo-stick jumping—but it's a number we can't help but be proud of and one we hope will still stand after this season's surfers have all come and gone.

The Berm

Dear Chuck Newby: Congratulations on moving to Steamboat. Before you wantonly disregard societal norms and revel in Mount Werner's bounty, there is one small thing you should know about living in Steamboat. It's called...The Berm.

They could make a horror flick about it, with a catchy title like The Berm That Ate Steamboat. The Berm makes the Blob whine like a little girl.

Sure, your pulse rate will rise and you'll make plans to blow off work the next morning when you see snowflakes blanketing your deck at night. You'll pre-load the car and coffee maker, line up your ski clothes in a nice little row, pack a PBJ and head to bed early. You won't even schmack the snooze alarm at 7 a.m.; you'll get up instantly, grogginess be damned. You'll forego a shower, wolf down some Oatmeal Squares and switch from your skivvies into your skiwear for your first powder day on the slopes. Then you'll fire up your Subaru, scrape its windshield with a CD case, and back down the driveway en route to a day of unbridled bliss.

That's when you'll see it. You'll notice it looming in your

peripheral vision at first, but it won't really register—something odd and amiss at the driveway's bottom. Only when you're almost upon it will come into full stomach-knotting view.

All that snow piled atop Steamboat is also piled in the streets, and the plows don't care about your powder habit. The result: A Great Wall of China blocking your access to the goods. You're so close and yet so far from your anticipated face shots. You might as well have the Broncos' offensive line crouching between you and Gate D.

Since it's churned up by Steamboat's finest, forget all about your little five-horsepower snowblower. The only way through is elbow grease, one vertebrae-piercing shovel-load at a time. You'll try to apply proper weight-lifting protocol and bend your legs with every heave. But soon you'll revert to using nothing but back to clear a path to the world on the other side of the wall.

You'll likely do a commendable job your first time. It might make you miss your gondola meeting, but your perfectly sculpted cleft will extend from bank to bank, a Moses-like parting of the Red Sea. Despite the fact that it made you miss first tracks, you'll step back with pride and marvel at your creation. You'll pat yourself on your aching back that a little manpower is all it took to thwart the combination of man's technology and nature's bounty.

Satisfied with a job well done, then you'll head out to the slopes, with the only real repercussion—aside from your back feeling like it's already banged down White Out—being that you have to cross tracks on your first run.

And all will be fine until you get home that night and see that it's still snowing. At first your mind won't really notice what this means; today's ski day will erase all memories of the morning's ordeal. But then you'll wake up the next morning and it will be there smiling at you all over again.

Like a recurring nightmare, it's The Return of the Berm and it's waiting to wreak havoc on any vertebrae left standing. That's when you'll mutter your first curse words at the beast. And that's when you'll truly know what it's like to be a local—especially after it happens over and over again, as if the plow drivers have a personal vendetta against you.

Our advice? Use your profanity sparingly...you'll need every Berm blasphemy you know to get you through the rest of the season.

Cat On A Hot Tin Roof

Science teachers: Want a case study for your next class? Use my house.

It all started on Valentine's Day when my 5-year-old niece, Lily, visiting with her parents from Alaska, came into the laundry room and told her mom, Laurie, she "was scared of the fire."

There was ample cause, with the emphasis on "amp."

When Laurie came out to the living room, sparks were flying, and not from her Valentine's affection toward her husband, Nino. They were arcing out the back of our freestanding gas stove, without rhyme or reason. Prudently turning the gas off, she then called us to come home from our cross-country ski outing to rectify matters.

When we arrived, the stove sat benignly in the corner. Even when we poked our heads around the stove's back, it was normalsville. No reason for all the huss and fuss, nor for us to have cut our outing short. But then came the rockets red glare. Buzz! Zap! it sputtered, sending sparks a flying.

Our first thought: Duh, unplug it. But there was no plug; it's a gas stove with no electrical component. While we knew this, we double-checked anyway before calling the stove guy.

"It can't be sparking," he echoed. "It only has a tiny AA battery for the igniter."

"Well, it is," I replied, both of us dumbfounded.

As Murphy would have it, we had more guests arriving that night, and we needed a warm house. Even my handyman neighbor Bob, who I waved in from outside, was perplexed.

The only thing the stove guy could offer was that maybe a wire was shorting out on the stove pipe or gas line. So we crawled around in the attic's insulation and basement cobwebs, to no avail.

Reasoning it was now a job for an electrician, we began the next round of calls to Steamboat sparkies. First Don, then Geoff, then Campo, all out of town on the Front Range. Then two more messages elsewhere. Don't electricians work on Fridays anymore? Finally, I hit pay dirt with White Out Electric, which happened to be in the neighborhood. "It's sparking?" they echoed.

My own electrical synapses fired when I walked onto our porch, still perplexed. That's when I noticed the electrical wires leading to our house hanging lower than normal. Sizzling sheet metal, I thought, maybe the entire roof was hot!

Sure enough, looking closer we saw that the year's epic snowfall had slid off our metal roof, bending our steel electrical mast 90 degrees, hidden by the snow overhang still clinging to our roof. It didn't take Ben Franklin to figure out who to call next: YVEA. Get someone over here, I said, before we start barbecuing birds.

They arrived like the cavalry, marching inside to the spark-throwing stove. Innocent-looking at first, it then sparked like something out of Poltergeist as soon as they neared, giving even the pros pause. They watched their voltmeter swing up to 120V when they held it to the stovepipe.

One of the house's two 120V wires had somehow turned our metal roof into a giant conductor. Taking the path of least resistance, the virus-like voltage then shot across the roof to our four-inch stove pipe, which it zipped down like a super-charged Santa. There, like running into General Patton's troops, it was stymied by a lone ceramic washer on the stove, designed to prevent heat from radiating up the pipe. All the curent could do now was hang out like snowboarders at a bar, looking for any sort of opening. The electric arcs it threw out—perhaps toward the metal runners of our nearby, antique sled—were its vain attempt to reach ground.

On the bright side, said Bob, at least it was all bypassing our meter. "Too bad we can't tap into it," he professed. "That's free power."

After YVEA shut it down, we got to work, ridding the roof of its remaining snow with 10-foot raft oars before turning things over to the still-incredulous pros. Soon the current was back where it belonged.

No sooner than YVEA flipped the switch on again and the doorbell (yes, electric) rang from our guests, one of whom was a design engineer as amazed as everyone else.

That's when I learned some electrical facts that I had forgotten since high school. One, it's insidious and, like a teen, has a mind of its own. Two, power (watts) equals current (40 amps) times volts (120V), meaning we had nearly 4.8KW bee-lining across our roof, enough to roast any robin (arc welders, my engineer guest added, often start with 3KW).

He also explained that if we were wearing shoes and standing on our carpet, we likely wouldn't have gotten shocked. But it would have been pure zapsville had we touched it standing barefoot after a shower on the stove tiles.

"The stove company is going to be proud of the design, even though that's not at all what it was intended for," he added. "You don't design a stove to handle your roof becoming electrified."

Had the high-amp urchins-of-electrons somehow bypassed Patton's washer, they would have charged the stove and followed the gas pipe into the ground. Touch it then and we'd likely feel a "little ting," he said, the hooligans happy with their existing ground source.

Still, it was a frightening reminder of what can happen when a snowball has a chance in hell. Replies rang the same from all the electricians I talked to, ranging from "You're kidding" to "It what?" Yet throughout all the mishaps of the mischievous electrons, it was Lily who proved the smartest one of us all.

Cody's Cardio Challenge

As I learned in Cody's Challenge, an uphill/downhill randonee ski race held in honor of former Steamboat ski patroller Cody St. John, there are countless ways to lose time in the trenches of competition. Especially if it's your first-ever time participating in such a cardiac-arresting contest.

I'd skinned and backcountry toured plenty. I'd just never raced, having people behind and ahead breathing down your neck.

For starters, you can lose time by being out of shape. You can also see the seconds, and minutes, tick away by being spastic at transitions—not getting your skins on or off quickly, or stepping into your tech binding incorrectly. And you can be slow on the downhills and cluster with layering, all time-suckers taking you farther and farther away from the winner's table.

So I punted early. With nearly 3,500 feet of climbing in store, I decided to make it my own personal Cody's Tour, not a race. I'd go at my own pace, without leaving a lung on the trail.

But I still wanted to put my best foot forward. So the weight-saving tactics began the night before. While I didn't drill holes into my headphones like my friend Pete professed, I did what I could. Instead of touring in Volants ("Ski the steel, steal the thunder") with anvils of boots like Lange Banshees, I had Dynafit skis, bindings and skins, with Garmont boots. For me, the whole package came in pretty light at 10.2 lbs. per leg (yes, I weighed it). But even that paled to racers using Dynafit's lightest racing set-up, which clocks in at a feathery 3.6 lbs. per quad.

I filled up my water reservoir only three-quarters full and pared down my pack, even taking out Band-Aides. I thought about not wearing underwear, but figured the ensuing rash would weigh more than my boxers.

Some people weren't as concerned with weight. On the gondola taking us to the race's start at the top of Thunderhead Lodge, one racer's dreadlocks weighed more than some racers' skis. And Ed Briones carried a boom box, salami log and 12-pack of PBRs in his pack.

This full spectrum was spread out at the starting line, from first-timer John Cosik, who heard about the race only the night before, to Olympic dignitaries Nelson Carmichael and Carolyn Lalive and logo-clad members of the U.S. Randonee Team (yes, there is such a thing).

The mass start started before I was ready, but at least I had my skis on, unlike the poor sap next to me. With one lycra-clad psycho taking off skating, I quickly realized there were two types of competitors: actual racers, clad in sponsor-covered one-pieces, and people like me, out to just have fun.

I also quickly learned that the race's incessant trudging offered a lot of time to ponder things—like how much time dropping and retrieving my visor cost me, and if the blister forming on my heel created more weight? Did the fog condensing on my sunglasses weigh more? Did every sip of water actually lighten my load, or simply move weight from one bladder to another? More importantly, would the weight loss from urinating make up for the lost time stopping?

Then came the transitions, which outweighed any lost time from these musings. At the top of a climb, you have to take your skins off, store them, switch your bindings to ski mode, and then schuss away. My technique: kick the ski tip up, peel off the skin, fold it up, stuff it in your shirt, and repeat. The key is not taking your ski off, saving you valuable click-in time; not clustering with changing layers; and not letting your skin get stuck to anything during the folding process.

At the bottom of the ski, you then have to reverse the whole process—usually only a few minutes later. This has the added dimension of having to take your skis off, unless you're the rare contortionist who can put skins on with skis still underfoot. This also means trying to click your boots back into your sometimes stubborn tech-binding toe-pieces, whose two little prongs have the painstaking habit of not aligning correctly. But at least my tribulations weren't as bad as the girl who accidentally put one skin on backward, making it stick going forward. Or Pete, who took his skins off in the flats when he shouldn't have, only to instantly have to put them on again to face another climb.

Switching your heel lifts can also devour the hourglass. Do it right and you can save energy and time. Flail at the intricate, pole-tip maneuver and the seconds pass along with fellow racers. You also have to weigh their geometric advantage. Is it worth the time to micro-shift from high to medium rise when the slope slackens, or better to have your quads burn from wearing high heels on the flats? You have to plot a graph, energy saved vs. time required, to assess which is fastest in the long run (not that you're anywhere close to running).

Come downhill time, you can make up time by pointing your skis down the fall line, but what you'll save is peanuts compared to climb time. Are the extra few seconds gained from Hahnenkamming it worth an Agony of Defeat? With conditions bullet-proof and littered with knee-jarring and binding-releasing ice-chucks, it was a balancing act in more ways than one (Ed kept his skins on to descend a glistening Cyclone, which proved a faulty decision).

By the time I peeled my skins off for the final time and schussed down to the finish at Slopeside Grill—lifting my ski tip to trigger the wand—I finished in the middle of the road, right about where my puke landed. My time of 2:19 was an hour off the winning time posted by some guy named Bjorn (actually Max Taam), placing me firmly back where I belonged with all the Joes, Petes and Bobs.

And in the end I realized that none of my ounce-saving savvy or even finish time really mattered anyways. Whether you're carrying a boom box or shaving chest hairs, Cody would be proud that you're out there.

Crustmongers Among Us

Save for pie, society isn't too big on crust. Pizza crust gets left in the box; toast crust gets directed to the disposal; and morning-crusted eyes get rubbed clean, Sandman be damned. And when the mountain crusts over, skiers head for brunch and a bloody mary.

But one aspect of this monosyllabic medium contradicts this. That's when a perfect crust forms on the spring snowpack atop Rabbit Ears Pass, serving up something relatively unique to Steamboat and its high-altitude flats: crust skiing.

It doesn't happen every day, week, month or even year. To get it, you need a series of warm, sunny days followed by clear, cold nights, all of which conspires to turn the once-soft snowpack into a giant popsicle. The keys are warm and cold. It has to get warm enough to create water in the snowpack, and cold enough for it to freeze and bond together, keeping you happily on the surface. Miscalculate either way and you might as well skate ski through crème brûlée.

Nail these perfect conditions and you're still not finished. You also have to time it right. The early bird gets the workout, which usually means rallying in the magic window between 6 a.m. and 10 a.m. The earlier you arrive the more frozen the snowpack, but the harder it is on every ankle muscle you never knew you had. Show up or stay out too late and your punishment is punching through.

While it's not an exact science, it still is one. There are crustmasters among us who study it diligently, waiting to pounce at the right conditions. They monitor temperatures, weather patterns, cloud cover, evaporation rates and their own intuition like a broker does stocks and bonds. And when the skate skiing stars align, they're up there daily, milking meadows for every herring bone track they're worth.

There's reason for the obsessive-like rallies. It's finite. The conditions can disappear as quickly as they arrive. One snowstorm or overnight warm spell and it's sayonara skate ski season. And too many sunny days suncup the surface like dimples on a golf ball. Even the most ardent, skate skiing soothsayer is never quite sure when their last outing will be.

Get it right, however, and you're in for one of Steamboat's true treats and most unsung sport. While everyone else is oiling bike chains and hanging up ski gear, the 10,000-foot topography becomes a pallet letting you glide anywhere you want to. Adios, eight-foot-wide groomed trails confining you all season and hello coloring outside the lines. It's like a kid getting his first bike, leaving boundaries in the dust.

The trick is finding open areas. Venture into thick timber and you're in for a grovelfest. It's a giant game of Connect the Meadows. You follow the perimeter of whatever open finger you find, and then foray through the forest to the next one. Some crazed crust skiers even use Google Earth to pinpoint meadows.

This breed of backcountry Nordic skiing also offers features you won't find at any Nordic center. You can skate ski up and over giant mounds, follow mini ridgelines and ramp-like wells, and soar alongside slowly awakening creeks. It turns usually cardio-centric skate skiing into an actually fun sport with moves to attempt, like rock climbing or running rapids. It can also be the fastest conditions you'll ski all year, the frozen crystals needing no special wax at all.

You just can't get too greedy. Nothing perfect lasts forever, and the same holds true for crust skiing. Like Cinderella staying out past midnight, push the day too far and things can get as gloppy as pumpkin innards.

And sometimes even the experts get hosed, breaking through the snow as soon as they step outside of their car. Despite all of their meticulous predictions, their hopes to skate ski sink with their skis. But for every one of those there's a time when they nail it, lengthening the season after the groomed trails have long melted away. And it's then that the crustmongers among us relish yet another reason to live in Ski Town USA.

Dorky Lines

"Excuse me, do you know where I can find any dorky lines?"

The man rolling down his car window while dropping his daughter off at Strawberry Park Elementary is a friend, but it doesn't dampen the dorkiness I feel from the question. It's become my calling card, and one of which I'm not particularly proud.

What, exactly, constitutes a dorky line? That's a question that comes later in the day from a ski patrol friend. Though you won't find them in any guidebook, the answer, in a nutshell, is threefold: high visibility tracks, easy accessibility and a maximum 15 turns. They're those lines around town that no one else in their right mind thinks of, largely because they're too...dorky.

Some are next to buildings, others thread their way down to softball fields. Some tally 10 turns, others only five after bushwhacking through scrub oak. They've even earned such names as the Hamburglar Couloir and Big and Little Gulp. Examples include the gradual slope below the Grand Summit, the north-facing steps at the rodeo grounds, even the power line coming off Emerald that crosses the skate-skiing tracks.

What they all share is accessibility and visibility. Townies can see the tracks returning home from work, joggers can see them from the bike path and parents can ogle them when returning from day care.

They're the type, say, that you might see from your workplace window and decide to bag at lunch. And, unfortunately, they're the type that can hypothetically cause your name to be broadcast to media outlets across the country, invoking long-lost friends to post Facebook messages linking to an AP story alongside the statement, "Looks like Eug is still getting after it."

It all started innocently enough one Thursday afternoon when I got a call from snowboard buddy Johnny St. John at work at the Little Red House on Oak Street. "Want to go bag a few dorky lines during lunch?" he asked. If ever there was a bountiful snowfall year to pursue them this was it, with a record November and near-record December and January. Next thing you know, we're trudging up the east face of the North Emerald Couloir, with base camp support vehicles stationed 40 vertical feet below the arête-flanked summit. We even came up with an acronym to support our mission: DORKs (Dads On ReKon).

Warm temperatures had annihilated the snowpack, but not before we descended the peak's precipitous northwest ridge. Adrenaline-addled, we then went for the crown jewel: the Double Z face, akin to Ed Viesturs bagging two 8,000-meter peaks, Lhotse and Everest, on the same expedition. We glassed it from the road, scouted our line—including a mandatory air off a rock-lined cornice—and then ascended once again, without even any supplemental oxygen.

We planned our ski and skied our plan. Everything went fine until my third turn—which happened to be about halfway down—and the slope let loose. Though I've seen bigger sloughs in my sugar bowl, the slope fractured into a Mini Me of an avalanche, wiping out our tracks. While we had planned to dine on the Double Z deck after work, toasting our sinuous curves, our itinerary vanished with the snow now lying in a debris pile at the slope's bottom.

That would have been the end of it, our dorky line dying in peace, were it not for a local reporter who caught wind of our exploits and ran a stop-the-presses piece on page two of the paper the next day. "Buchanan and St. John have formed a midday habit of looking for a little powder during the lunch hour," the piece read. "They ski on small slopes they describe as 'dorky lines.' As they came over the ridge and around a small fir tree, the slope let loose. Neither of them were caught or injured in the slide, which broke away below them and slid about 60 feet down the western edge of the Howelsen Hill area. Wet-slab avalanches are most likely to occur during warm weather when the snowpack doesn't freeze hard during the night. It creates instability between the layers of snow, and the lower layer no longer is able to support the layer above…"

He might not have taken twenty-seven color eight-by-ten photographs with circles and arrows on them as happened to Arlo Guthrie in Alice's Restaurant, but he did call in an avalanche expert who rated the slide a one on a scale of five, and even secured a second source from the Colorado Avalanche Information Center. "The fracture line was not smooth," the story read, "indicating cohesion among the grains of snow was low."

Our infamy would have stayed confined to town had the same reporter not posted it to the wire. Denver's Channel 4 and 9 News picked it up the next day, and the Associated Press distributed it across the country. "Urban Avalanche!" the headlines blared, reciting testimony from the avalanche expert. Then Brian Harvey's Pirate and Yesterday newspaper parodied the piece, showing a photo of a snowboarder upside-down in a trash dumpster after riding "dorky lines off downtown rooftops into trash bins." They called me BlueJean Youcannon and expounded upon how the landing-zone dumpsters had become dense and unstable.

As with Steve Martin finally making the phone book in The Jerk, I like to think that you've made it in life when you get parodied in a paper. But chagrin comes with such celebrity. You field embarrassing questions when dropping your daughter off at school; live with demeaning nicknames like Urban Sluff, which a Howelsen Hill ski patrol still calls me to this day; and you get on your college buddies' radars again, not from a notice in an alumni magazine about getting your PhD but from skiing a sophomoric ski line.

Of course, even dorkdom has a silver lining. "Look at it this way," said a friend after watching the results from the Olympics in Torino. "At least you satisfied the Steamboat media vacuum from the Olympics."

Fear and Loathing with Snow Blowers

I approach it with trepidation every year—you never know what kind of reaction you're going to get after ignoring it so long.

No, I'm not talking about my dog after a long absence, or even a visit to my doctor or dentist. It's something far more crucial to living in a mountain town: my snow blower.

Every winter, I put it off as long as possible. The first couple of storms I'll convince myself it's good to have packed-down snow covering the driveway; it keeps the gravel from churning up into the auger. I'll feebly compact snow strips with my car and shovel high-use areas to avoid the larger, more-looming task. But I know I'm just plugging the dike with my finger. All the while, my wife watches the driveway's height rise inch by packed-down inch.

I can get away with it for smaller storms, the two- to three-inchers. But eventually the Big Kahuna lands, requiring the inevitable visit to the shed. This year I made it all the way to December 13, a near record.

I'm not sure why I prolong it; it's not like it's a visit to the proctologist. It's likely just years of neglected upkeep—knowing I'll pay in shoulder-dislocating cord pulls and, like the above doctor visit, a series of sputtering coughs. Then, invariably, I'll load it into the car to visit to the repair guy again.

But not this time. This year, like Charlie Brown about to knock it out of the park, I'm going to succeed. It's going to fire-up on the first pull and roar to life, just like winter has.

Knowing I've lost the snow pack-down battle, I squeak open the door and peak inside. There it is, a dog chained to its leash, waiting to romp in the snow. Still, if history is any indication, I'm doomed. Most years that lawnmower-pulling move I occasionally do on the dance floor is all in vain. Or I'll get the bait-and-switch, a false positive. It'll roar to life, luring me to place it into action too soon. I'll throw up that first plume of powder only to see it stall halfway down the drive.

But this year I have a few aces up my sleeve. While I know you have to drain it of gas at the end of each season, it's taken me 20 years to learn you also have to let it run itself dry afterward. So said the repair guy during last year's visit, a ritual as regular as receiving Aunt Daphne's fruit cake. He also advised using ethanol-free gas to replace the five-year-old fuel in my can (even though that gas powers our $50 lawnmower fine, without all the witchcraft involved).

So I'm rightfully apprehensive. But lo and behold, after four delicate primer pushes, moving the throttle from turtle to rabbit, and turning the choke—a little, but not too much, then back off again—my Craftsman 5.0 coughs to life on the second pull, glenohumeral joint intact. It's purring like our cat, Rufus, and wagging its tail like our dog, Java.

Re-learning which lever is the auger and which is for propulsion, like General Patton leading the U.S. Third Army in the Allied Invasion of Normandy, I concoct a plan of attack. Start in the middle of the driveway, not the outside (duh), and don't bother with the areas I already shoveled. Then comes deciding which bank to throw snow to first and angling the shooter for the best trajectory. Then I start my first lap.

The first sweep's snow from the lone stripe down the middle won't reach the far bank—which is demoralizing, knowing I'll have to re-blow it. But there's no alternative, so I plug on. I also have to calculate how much to overlap each lane. Get greedy and scoop the full blade width and I'll have to re-blow the leftover ridge. But taking only half means more laps.

After a while, I get in the zone, cherishing the little engine that could. Admittedly, its 179cc, forfeit-my-Man-Card size is grossly under-horsed for our 1,500-square-foot driveway. But a bigger one could just mean bigger problems, which I have enough of with this one. Oops, sorry about that piece of gravel, little buddy, and that mangled tennis ball. Collateral damage.

I forget to re-angle the thrower away from the open shed door, plastering everything inside. Sorry, rakes. At the bottom, I throw snow onto an overhanging branch, dumping more on my head. Then I go too far into a bank, making our driveway look like Italy. But I don't go too far into the street; I'll leave that for the city.

Up top, I barely make the turn before careening into the wooden porch steps, a scar I'd remember all summer. Then I head back down, widening and widening the white stripe.

After the last plume flutters onto the bank, I steer my trusty, snow-throwing steed back into the shed, releasing the auger just before splintering the door jam. Then I switch it off and all's quiet. I've done it. The inaugural monkey's off my back for another season.

I turn and look at my work with pride. But like the monks who make those artsy sand mandalas only to throw them to the wind, it's a fleeting masterpiece. The next storm's snowflakes are already starting to fall.

Finagling Powder

When storms roll through town like the one last week —which dumped 36 inches atop Mount Werner—it means dusting off your skis and snowboards, but also something else: your powder clause at work, one of the key benefits of living in a mountain town. But there's an art to it to ensure your bosses—at work and on the home front —don't perceive you as shirking your duties.

Like Clark Kent turning into Superman, you often have to go incognito. Not in the phone booth sense, but in being sly nonetheless. Which means breaking out some age-old hooky-playing techniques. Like the old leave-the-house-and-drop-the-kids-off-at-school-in-your-work-clothes trick, so your spouse doesn't suspect anything and your kids can't rat you out. While it means still having to change somewhere, most likely in the parking lot, it keeps your cover clean.

If you happen to venture into the office beforehand—good because you're seen there; bad because you have to sneak back out—it's time for a different set of shams. The old drape-your-coat-on-the-back-of-your-chair trick works well, luring workmates into thinking you're simply in the bathroom or getting coffee. You can augment the deception by angling the chair out just so (not tucked in under your desk), leaving your desk light on, and scattering papers about next to a cup of coffee. Another trick: drop a piece of dry ice into your coffee for perpetual, I'm-just-in-the-bathroom steam. Even the Daily Bugle's Jonah Jameson would buy that alibi.

On the slopes, your only fear of discovery is bumping into your workmates or, worse, boss, in which case you're all in the same boat. Just don't forget to carry on the ruse after your schralping session. This means keeping work clothes at the ready to change back into at the car— entailing standing on the floor mat in the parking lot, sitting on a grocery bag to keep your butt off the wet bumper, and quicko-presto stripping down to your boxers to pull on your Kuhls. Sometimes, you might leave your longjohns on, which makes your ensuing office time warm but minimizes public exposure.

Then you fix your collar and tie your shoes (like a goggle tan, loose laces are a dead give-away), and run your hands through your helmet hair to eliminate tell-tale coifs off to the side. Façade complete, next you check your texts, messages and emails, hoping none were overly time sensitive, and beeline back to the grind, no one the wiser. It might even call for throwing a sideways hand over your face if you see a family member or fellow employee at an intersection.

The only alternative to the parking lot change is to switch back into your civilians back home, which adds time to your awayness, or to do so at work, inviting the unwanted risk of discovery. For that, you sneak in the employee-only door and head straight to the john, where you swap ski for street clothes, perhaps even hiding out in the stall. Then you have to get rid of the evidence, either stashing your ski clothes bag somewhere inside, like that nook by the trashcan, or shuttling it back to your car—where you realize your car-topped skis or board could also give you away. But at least that's circumstantial, and would never hold up in court.

Do it right and about the only way to get busted is if anyone recognizes the Boar's Head sandwich with the Gondola Joe's wrapper that you eat at your desk, or the similarly logo'd latte cup. And, of course, you ruin every painstaking step you took to cover your tracks by posting a Instagram photo of the ones you left on the mountain.

The First Skate

It's done, and I survived: the first skate ski of the season.

The annual rite of passage usually occurs on Bruce's Trail atop Rabbit Ears Pass. And it happens 1) earlier than it does anywhere else in the country, meaning you're not in shape for it; and 2) at 10,000 feet, meaning you're really not in shape for it. All this is why it's usually met with the trepidation, say, of having the in-laws visit.

The trail doesn't need much snow to open; some years it's as early as October—right in the heart of football-watching, couch-potato season. Meticulously groomed like Jimmy Fallon's hair, all it needs is six to eight inches for the snow machine to pack out its two circular laps. A second storm usually makes it good to go for as long as they groom it (until the valley's Nordic centers open).

For that brief period it's the only game around, a winter wonderland stacked right up against the end of bike season. All you need is your gear and gumption.

And lungs. Its altitude is also its bane; you feel it on your first stride, while remembering how to balance on toothpicks. Master elevation and equilibrium and you still have the route to deal with, which serves up its own peculiarities.

First comes crossing a tiny bridge, hoping you don't end up in the drink. The next hurdle is getting up the first hill to the groom machine shed. It's not much, but enough to remind you it's been a long time since you've unleashed your inner Sven.

Thankfully, a fortuitous trail junction awaits, letting you rest under the guise of congregating. It was here, hunched over my poles, where I lingered with eight, decaled members of the Steamboat Springs Winter Sports Club, also out for one of the season's first skates.

"Uh, you guys go ahead," I offered, my Darwin senses kicking in.

From there, it was onto the flats before decision time: the flatter, weenier short lap or more manly and hilly big lap? Naturally, I choose the latter, soon finding myself careening down toward Hairball Corner, a lefthand hairpin that's a true test of off-season spasticness. I stepped-turn my way around it as if walking on stilts, bypassing a fellow early-seasoner dusting himself off next to a body divot in the snow.

The next hill was the real morale and ego killer, red-lining my heart rate until it matched the magenta alpenglow.

Hill climbed, I began to get into the groove. The loop flattened, letting me ponder between pole plants (one of which landed between my legs). I mulled my instant immersion into winter, what beetle-stricken trees had fallen, and how my pathetically waxed my skis were.

The reprieve was short-lived. Soon, I slowed to a crawl and began herring-boning up yet another hill without a hint of glide. At top came a natural rest stop, where I briefly contemplated taking the short cut to the shorter loop. But that's copping out, so I continued along the main loop—easier with more downhills, but a butt-kicker nonetheless.

Here, I experimented with V1ing, V2ing and V-whatevering again, all while pushing my VO-max levels. Finally, I emerged panting and beaten at the confluence of the big and little loops, where it was decision time: hit the big one again or swallow my pride go short? Thinking I'd cave if I didn't bag it now, I went big once more time before finishing the shorter loop in near darkness, now skiing by Braille. On Nov. 11, it officially gets dark at 5:26 p.m.

The important thing is I got the monkey off my back— at least until next year.

The First Skin

Whether it's trudging up Mount Werner before the resort opens or breaking trail in the backcountry, donning skins and earning your turns is ascending in popularity just like its minions are doing on mountains.

But it involves skills and equipment far removed from summer's bikes, paddleboards and pogo sticks. And assuming you have the requisite boots, bindings and skis, either tele or AT, it means rounding it all up again before your first step.

First comes finding where you stashed it all summer, especially your skins, whose molasses-like glue hopefully didn't collect safety pins, thumbtacks and hairballs during storage. Then comes re-enlisting your skis, poles and boots after their hibernation. Unfortunately, they're all just how you left them, last spring's "I'll fix it" vow as empty as your pocketbook after making your season pass payment.

You hold up your pants to find the same hole and zipper broken. Your ski bottoms are still caked with mud and leaves from June's 14er, and your pole basket is duct-taped together with a wicket. And there are new issues to deal with also, like sliding your foot into your boot to find that mice have squirreled cat food in its toe.

Gear set—which can also include avi gear if you're heading into the backcountry—it's time to head out, where the real fun begins.

Chore number one: applying the skins, a skill lost over the summer. First comes the Herculean task of pulling them apart after they've bonded together all summer; it almost dislocates your shoulder before the season even begins. Next comes putting them on. Different skins require different techniques, some starting at the tail and others the tip. All require an even base-pressing to eliminate wrinkles and precision placement, like coloring between the lines, so you don't cover one edge while exposing the other. And heaven forbid, don't put them on backwards so they stick going forward and slide back downhill.

Next up: fitting your boots into your bindings. While not really an issue with tele or AT frame bindings, it is with today's tech bindings. You have to free your boot holes of coagulants, line them up just right and then utter some magic juju for the tell-tale click.

Now's when you turn on your tunes—hopefully something more uplifting than He Aint' Heavy's "It's a long, long road..."—and start trudging. And you reacquaint yourself with the one-step-after-another mantra proving biking shape doesn't equal hiking shape.

If you're on teles, now another task surfaces: remembering to put your bindings into "tour" mode, another modern convenience complicating things. But the free-swinging heel is worth it, so you pry the gizmo open.

Nine steps in, you likely have to take off a layer, something you should have done from the start. So you take off your pole straps, gloves and pack and strip down, realizing heat management skinning is just as important as it is in the hot springs.

After 30 steps, the incline steepens and another factor comes into play: remembering how to flick up your heel lifts again. While you might've had the pry-and-twist or basket-flip move dialed last spring, that muscle memory has long since disappeared. Sometimes that little thingy spins too far back into lock mode or gets stuck in no man's land. Regardless, the energy it saves is worth the cluster, even if you eschew aesthetics and awkwardly stoop over to lift it with your hand.

Now the real trudging begins. The first few strides aren't so bad; you actually feel pretty good. But by step 100, monotony kicks in. That's when you make the mistake of looking up and seeing how far away the top still is. So you let your mind wander, or if you have a partner and the cardio-ability, you talk, or at least listen. Or you groove to your tunes, wondering when that Geico ad will interrupt Pandora. Whatever you do, you don't focus on that hot spot forming on your ankle.

If you've been on the route before, say to the top of Thunderhead or Mount Werner, you'll anticipate every flat spot that requires you to mess with your lifts again, and every icy steep pitch, where you're forced to delicately weight your poles each step to prevent the dreaded, energy- and ego-draining back slip.

Persevere and you'll make it, just before pulmonary edema settles in. Now, all you have to do is throw a layer back on so your sweat doesn't freeze and take your skins off. This can be done the cool way with your skis still on— employing either the tip or tail up trick—but in the end, why bother? Someone in your group will take their pack and skis off, requiring you to wait anyway.

But at least this gives you more time to fold your skins up perfectly glue-to-glue again, which will likely take four tries, the last of which will be barely better than your first. Then you stuff them in your jacket or pack (the jacket keeps the glue warmer) and shove off to reap your hard-earned reward: those turns, hopefully powder, that you'll cherish more than any chair-accessed arcs you'll make all season. As long, of course, as you remembered to put your heel lifts back down before skiing away.

Getting Valeted

"I wonder if they get a commission on them?" asks my friend the Anonymous Realtor. "Sort of a bounty?"

"Maybe a different amount for skis and boots," I proffer.

We're at the Sunset Happy Hour put on by the Steamboat Ski Area at the top of the mountain and we've been outsmarted by security. Our ski boots have been courteously "valeted" for us down the gondola.

We'd heard that the resort didn't want people skinning up the mountain, attending Happy Hour, and then skiing down inebriated. For good reason. Schussing on suds doesn't sit too well with one's liability insurance. Their solution: have security "valet" your skis down, forcing any patrons who skinned up to ride the gondola down.

While we weren't planning to drink, we were hoping to ski what we had so painstakingly sweated up, after poking our heads in to see our friend's band. While it's sound policy by the resort, it's gray differentiating who's up there to get down on the dance floor and who's there to ski down Heavenly Daze.

When it comes to skinning, I'm in it for the cardio instead of the cocktail. We'd heard through the rumor mill that once up top, if you wanted to go inside and still ski down, you had to stash your skis. So we wore trousers under our ski pants and brought shoes so we looked like we came straight off Seventh Avenue. The only problem was there were five of us, easy pickings for the binocular-clad bouncers pacing the railing.

"Hey!" a guard yelled from the deck as if we were penetrating the German fortress in "Where Eagles Dare." "If you come inside, you can't ski down!"

We'd been compromised, no sooner than my buddy laid his skis against the building. We felt like we were in high school again, only we were 50-somethings trying to sneak into—and then back out of—a party. Not trying to scare up babes or beer, but simply the ability to ski down.

Naturally, with old habits dying hard, those of us who hadn't been seen snuck around the corner and changed into our civilians. Then we strolled in confidently, blending in with the other attendees. We even saw our compromised buddy, whose gear had already been graciously sent down. Bless his heart, he pretended he didn't know us to eliminate suspicion from the guards.

Soon we were absorbed by the packed-house revelry. And all was said and fine until, fifteen minutes later, our "valeted" buddy told us the grim news. "Dudes: I saw a guy walking by with two sets of boots and backpacks," he whispered. "He said, 'I found their boots, but not their skis.' It sounded like he was gloating."

Now we were compromised. Go straight to jail, do not pass Go, do not collect $200. It was Alcatraz time.

Venturing outside to ascertain the espionage, we cast errant eyes to our lair. Yep, our boots had been absconded. Damn, these guys were good. The vital link to our skis was gone, likely already lined up with the rest of the confiscated gear at the gondola base, like the Misfit Toys in Rudolph.

While my skis had also been courteously valeted, my Anonymous Realtor buddy's skis remained hidden. My only solace: I remained anonymous (at least until this confession) as I walked dejectedly back inside; at least the security folks didn't have the satisfaction of knowing whose gear they sent down. Not so my friend. Boots gone, he had to come back inside with his skis, forced to do the walk of shame in front of the guards.

"Have a nice run," they chastised, with a hint of hubris.

Then he walked over to join us, hand caught in the cookie jar.

At the bottom, our gear was waiting in a row against the wall, like a line-up at the police station. After all that hard work skinning up, we didn't get to ski down. But we had a helluva time with the war games.

Hogan's Heroes

"Hogaaaan!"

I can almost hear Colonel Klink's yell. I'm halfway through a seven-mile cross-country ski trail on Hogan Park from Rabbit Ears Pass to the top of Steamboat Ski Area. With only 800 feet of elevation gain, and wide, flat meadows to traverse, this gives my mind plenty of time to wander. Mine just so happens to do so toward the goofy TV show bearing the trail's name, one set in a bumbling German POW camp with the lovable and portly Schultz, easily bamboozled Klink and conniving Hogan.

I hadn't skied the trail for 16 years, and the show's heyday was another 16 before that. The last time was in 1998, just two years after the Morningside lift went in, which saves you the final climb.

Like Hogan sneaking out of camp, the timing seemed right to do it again: the mountain was skied out, the backcountry was shot from the season's second crust layer, and it was a beautiful day offering the much-needed visibility.

The first hurdle was figuring out our shuttle. Since you start at Rabbit Ears and end at the resort's base, you have to either leave your car and drive back up or, like Hogan, connive someone into helping. Let's see...who could we get to shuttle? My daughter Brooke readily volunteered, but only because she had her permit but not a license and wanted to drive alone. Sorry, honey. Perhaps my friend Shelli, who was driving to Denver? Nope, she already left. Then the lightbulb flashed. My buddy Arnie, who had just gotten knee surgery and was laid-up, but not so laid-up that he couldn't drive. Sitting home bored, he agreed for a six-pack.

Wingman Bob in place, next came the great gear debate. You want to go as light as possible, but not so light that you spaz out on the 3,000-foot descent from the ski area. So despite all the new school AT and other gear on the market, the best set-up turned out to be our oldest: our ancient tele gear, including jet-black Asolo Extreme leather boots and yellow, anorexic Tuas with pin-and-cable bindings, which I've kept, for some reason, for 20 years. Top this with equally old, knee-high purple gaiters straight out of the '80s and I was good to go.

Starting at about 9,200 feet and finishing at 10,023 at the base of Morningside, the trail heads north just east of the Walton Peak parking lot. That's where Arnie dropped us, leaving us with our next decision: wax. (Hint: skin it and you'll likely never do the route again.) For that, we went with good ol' Steamboat-style Extra Blue. Get it right and it's like you're moon-walking on a moving walkway, gliding ten feet every stride.

The only place it didn't truly shine was on the quick, 200-foot climb right out of the gate. A herring bone or two later, we emerged onto a pair of flat meadows before surviving a short, tree-lined descent to a sharp right across Fishhook Creek. Miss it and you're wallowing in Walton Creek Canyon. Luckily, on a clear day the trail's blue diamond markers are easy to see, picking up your spirits with each sighting. Just don't tackle the trail in a white-out; it has as many landmarks as Bismarck, North Dakota.

The creek crossing leads to the longest climb of the tour and another descent that tests your skinny ski stripes (note: avoid the tree at the hairpin). A few moonwalking meadows later and you join Hogan Creek, at which point, Hallelujah!, you can finally to see the Morningside lift. Just don't pop the champagne cork yet; it's farther away than it looks.

A few more meadow crossings and you're almost there, but you also lose reference in the thick trees. Tracks veer this way and that and you'll second-guess the proper route. The groveling soon ends, however, as you finally emerge from the woods into civilization (when we did, two ladies skiing the catwalk hooped and hollered at our garb).

Admittedly, we cut it a hair close. My watch read 2:55 p.m., with the lift closing at 3. One more pee stop and we would've faced a final few hundred-foot climb to the top of Buddy's Run. But we made it on and cracked a beer before trying to re-learn how to ski down on skinny gear. Yes, it is as hard as it looks. Picking the easiest way down that wouldn't completely compromise our manhood—at least we didn't take Why Not—we eventually made it back to the car we had dropped off earlier and finally home, where our gaiters, boots and red bandanas could be stowed away again, like Hogan's secret maps and radios, until next time.

A Hut Trip Hunch

Admittedly, it was an odd couple of items to bring on a winter ski hut trip. My ice skates barely fit in the pack's top and my hockey stick protruded above it like an elk antler.

"Dad, why are you bringing that?" asked my daughter, Casey, one of six kids along. "It's a ski trip."

Indeed, it was our annual family hut trip, one of the best things you can do with your kids. Pick an easy-to-get-to abode like we did—the Nohku and Agnes Creek huts off Cameron Pass—and fill it with like-minded families, and you have a winter get-away they'll remember forever.

They were already getting something to remember from my unorthodox packing list.

But I had a hunch. I'd been to this hut before and seen the ice on a high alpine lake above it Zamboni'd smooth by the wind. We'd just come off a bleak January in terms of snowfall and it had been windy for days. So I played my gut. Even though you're supposed to pack light on a hut trip, I splurged, bringing skates, a stick and a 5.8-ounce hockey puck.

No matter that the stick was a giant radar antennae protruding above my pack on the skin in, catching branches that others easily skied under. My premonition overruled pride.

We arrived at the huts by two-ish, settled in, ate lunch, and then headed up for our ice skate assault on the lake.

Hidden by a ridge during the climb up, the lake rests in an oasis-like basin just north of Rocky Mountain National Park, surrounded by the jagged pinnacles of the Crags and such peaks as Mount Richthofen and Mount Mahler. Ascending a gully, hockey stick rising above my pack like a flag, I began to have doubts. What if it was covered in snow? I estimated there was a 50-50 chance it would be clear.

My buddy Murph crested the ridge first, privy to its first look. I followed a few minutes behind. At first glance, I was disheartened. Its western end was blanketed in white. But then my eyes strayed eastward. Jackpot. Its entire left hand side was mirror smooth.

Traversing over to the ice's edge, I changed out of my ski boots and into my skates, ignoring the cold transition. Then I post-holed through the snow, my skates cutting deep trenches, and tentatively put blade to ice. Testing the surface's purchase like Bambi, I pushed off.

While I wasn't going to give Apolo Ohno a run, the aesthetics trumped all. Above towered a serrated ridgeline of peaks; below, three feet of see-through ice. It was hard to imagine any material on earth being clearer. White air bubbles coalesced through the ice like clouds, gathering at random after being burped up from the depths. Thin cracks crisscrossed here and there like fissures after an earthquake, but posed no threat to blade. Neither did slight, wave-like undulations on the surface. The open stretch of ice ran for 400 yards or so, the longest straight line I've ever skated. It was our own Mystery, Alaska, the rink's boards a towering backdrop of peaks.

After a few laps dribbling the puck around errant wisps of snow, I returned to our makeshift bench with a smile as wide as the arcs I left in the ice. One by one we traded off so everyone had the chance to skate, the big-footed among us squishing into my size 10s and the diminutive wadding up socks in the toes. It wasn't the exact fit that was important, but the experience. Mesmerized for longer than prudent, each participant unable to hold back a howl of jubilation, we returned to the hut just as the stars began to peer out of an ice-clear sky.

Then the normal hut trip routine resumed. We re-fueled with pre-made paella and coconut snow ice cream, played games (this time the card-to-your forehead HeadBands, somehow prompting the kids to always guess, "Am I a Bathroom?"), and finally turned in. And the next day we all went skiing, the main reason we came. But it paled to playing a hunch that paid off in blades.

Nokhu/Agnes Creek Hut Beta

Named for the Nokhu Crags towering just above it to the east, the Nokhu (no' koo) and Agnes Creek huts each sleep six and are located at 10,000 feet in the southern end of the Colorado State Forest State Park on the south side of Colorado Highway 14 about two miles west of Cameron Pass (about a hour and a half drive from Steamboat). The 1.5-mile skin in has a kid-friendly elevation gain of just 540 feet and takes about 45 to 60 minutes (snowmobiles aren't allowed). The two huts are separated by a stand of trees and share a common outhouse, but are within easy walking distance. Each cabin can also be rented individually (weekends: $110/night; weekdays: $90). Locals hint: If it hasn't snowed in a while, bring your skates.

An Inside Look at Ski Town Jobs

Let's face it: Unless you're a trust-funder or total dirtbag, moving to a ski town means getting a job. Even if you only make enough to score a pass, couch space and PBJ makings, you're not going to turn unless you earn.

The jobs you're likely to get—and that likely means more than one—run from teaching kids how to ski to playing lifeguard at lift lines. They all have their pros and cons, and take practice. At my first ski town job—tossing pizzas in Telluride—my early pies came out the shape of Texas and Oklahoma.

To investigate the matter, I went undercover, putting myself in a variety of ski town jobs under the guise of research. Convincing employers to let me work various positions covertly was the easy part. Actually doing the jobs was harder; being incognito meant jumping into their daily grind. Throughout it all, I was exposed to a day in the life of the average ski town employee—which should shed some light on what to expect from whatever trade you decide to ply.

Rental Clerk

Because I punched in at Steamboat Rentals at 3 p.m. on a powder day, everyone was more into swapping ski stories than working. Especially since the stories were coming from Eric, a first-year clerk who showed up for his shift with a tree branch in his hair, a ripped jacket, and a cut cheek. Therein lies one of the best aspects of working in a rental shop: You're on the front line, as close to skiing as you can get for a job that doesn't require being on the snow. "It's the job to have," said second-year clerk Cameron McGregor. "You get a pass and the time to use it."

Eric's tree-bashing stories didn't last long. With the 4,300-person National Brotherhood of Skiers expected to descend in full force, manager John Ward made sure all hands were on deck to prepare for the onslaught. "We should have our whole inventory of 1,200 packages rented out by tomorrow morning," he said as my eyes widened in fright. "You'll be a big help."

I don't know how much help I was. For the first hour I simply hung out behind the retail counter, the highlight of which was helping a lady pull a Hot Chilis top over her head. The neck was too tight, and I left her stumbling around looking like she was trying to hit a piñata. Next, John asked me to move a bunch of poles from the front rack to the back. Although it doesn't require a PhD., rental clerking isn't a complete no-brainer. While I was carrying poles every which way across my chest, I was lapped three times by Volker, a 21-year-old-surfer-turned-snowboarder who had just died his hair red to retaliate against ski corp. for making him cut it. His secret? Carry the poles by the straps.

From there I went to the boot-fitting arena, where again I showed signs of rental ineptitude: Since they came in identical bottles, I sprayed the first 20 pairs of boots with Windex instead of foot odor juice. Fitting boots was another matter. Volker told me it once took three clerks to snap a rear-entry boot shut on a five-foot-two, 260-pound woman: two pushing behind the calf and one ready with the latch. When the buckle finally latched, all three fell over.

Sizing skis is just as tough, boiling down to a game of wills: "I don't think you want a 210," I told a five-foot-four beginner. "Try these 160s." Usually their egos will give in. But they're still not above treating the skis as rentals. Volker once saw a customer put his skis on outside the front door and ski down a set of cement stairs.

Returns are easy to deal with, except there always seems to be more boots than there are racks. And getting hit on the head by a size 360 Salomon quickly teaches you not to squeeze in more than the rack will allow. As for skis, you simply give the bases a quick scan to see if their users have been skiing like Eric.

Bartending

Dean Goering, 31, a seven-year veteran at a bar called the Inferno, didn't waste any time. "So, did you ski today?" he asked the two girls who had just bellied up for Crown Royals and cokes. Giggling, they quickly launched into a story about the day. If a waitress hadn't needed a pitcher of Killian's he would have had a phone number.

Behind Dean's seemingly innocent question is the underlying benefit of bartending: the ability to flirt while on the clock. "It's great because you get to talk to girls," said barkeep Jim Meehan, 28. "Otherwise, you never get to do that in a ski town." He also said that it's the best money going—he'd pull in $75 in tips for the three-hour shift—and that you get to ski everyday. "Of course, you usually don't wake up until one or two," he added.

After 45 minutes on the job I could see his words held water—even if my liver didn't; Dean had already subjected me to a shot of Grand Marnier, a kamikaze and a '47 Cadillac, and he was fast approaching with another. And therein lies the inherent pitfall with bartending. It's hard not to get liquored-up with free booze staring you in the face.

No matter how buzzed you get, though, you still have a job to do, whether it's washing glasses, scrubbing counters or pouring drinks. And since I chose to work the Inferno's aprés shift, I had to be as on top of my game as a downhiller on the Hahnenkamm. With Ugly Kid Joe and two other grunge bands starting their "Excuse to Go Snowboard" Tour at 8 p.m., the place was already a zoo. To top it off, the bar was filled with ski instructors lining up for their free daily beer, and it was time to let someone spin the infamous shot wheel. Dean handed me the microphone and let me solicit an unsuspecting lass to do the honors. Carol's spin quickly earned 40-cent shots for the crowd, with one table wasting no time in ordering 150 of them.

When the aprés crowd died down it was time to restock, which takes as much balance as skiing bumps. Only there's no room for recoveries: Overloaded, I broke two bottles of beer while re-filling the coolers. Even with the restocking and dishwashing, however, bartending is a coveted position. And it's a tough job to get. Of five barkeeps, only one, Mike Petix (pronounced "P-tex"), was less than a two-year rookie. Charly, who showed up for the late shift, had been at it 11 years. And you could tell she had the scene wired. Even though she could barely hear over the noise (at one point the band yelled "Skiers suck!" prompting P-tex to flip it off), she patrolled the bar like a watchdog, cleaning counters and filling orders at breakneck speed. She didn't flirt as much as Dean, but then again, she didn't have to.

Bellhop

Contrary to popular belief, you don't have to wear a stupid-looking cap when you work as a bellboy. At the Steamboat Sheraton, where I was gainfully employed on St. Patrick's Day to help with 68 check-ins and check-outs, it was black pants, a maroon button-down shirt, and a bolo tie. It actually looked pretty cool.

Though I may have looked the part, however, the job was no cakewalk. The basic gist was easy: grab a luggage cart and follow people either to their rooms or out to a taxi. But even if you hauled around a red wagon as a kid, the finer details take some acclimation: Take corners wide so you don't divot hallways; carry a doorstop in your pocket to avoid holding doors open with your butt; and keep the swivel wheels toward you so you can control the damn thing.

I didn't start out batting a thousand. I got lost downstairs after getting my uniform and directed two people to the kitchen instead of the bathroom. I also didn't fare too well on the phone, especially since my nametag read Dave from Coshocton, Ohio. "Bell desk. This is Eugene…I mean Dave, can I help you?" One couple checking in even tried to make small talk by saying they were from a town nearby. My saving grace in blending in was that the two other bellhops were also named Dave: Dave Calicowski, who had been at it 11 years; and Dave Kiemig, a seven-year ski instructor/bellhop.

While they were running around helping people with bags, I busied myself with a bellhop's other duties: I helped a lady put film in her camera and answered such questions as "When is it going to snow next?" and "Where can I get my skis polished?" After a while, I too got into the bag business. My first job was playing Igor in waiting, following Dave No. 1 to Room 532 to carry down six suitcases. As soon as we got them downstairs the phone rang: they needed them back in their room so they could look for their plane tickets. In the elevator, Dave said things like that happen all the time. One guy from Germany, he added, even mistakenly showed up a year early for a symposium.

My first solo mission was carrying bags to Room 249, pushing the cart, swivel forward, behind a couple from Washington, D.C. I must have done halfway well because the guy handed me three bucks. And I must have looked the part because on the way back a cleaning lady pinched me on the butt because I wasn't wearing green.

All in all, it seemed a fairly laid-back position. "We actually have it pretty easy," said Dave No. 2 during a break in the action. "We're always helping people out, so everyone's nice to us." Of course, it could also be that people simply feel sorry for us: They've most likely seen the hats most bellhops have to wear.

Ski Tuner

After getting issued my apron, I walked into the Sharper Edge's tuning room and shut the door before the music could escape into the retail room. Next to the WinterSteiger Micro1, the world's most advanced ski-tuning machine, Dan Vandevender, a 33-year-old ex-racer with a gash across his right index knuckle, was holding a ski across his stomach, air-guitaring to Frank Zappa's "Dynamo Hum." As soon as his riff was done, he finished running the ski through the machine.

Tunes and tuning, I found, go hand in hand. In the corner was a five-disc CD player that owners and ex-USSA racers Gary Cogswell and Tom Olden had purchased to keep their tuners tuning. Gary turned it down enough to walk me through the ropes. "You're looking at a Ferrari," he yelled over the noise of the grinder and CD player. "It can do anything you want done to a ski—digital edge grinding, base beveling, and any base-structure you want." Fifteen dials on the control panel backed up his claim. So did the 150 pairs of brand new Aspen S skis leaning against the ski posters on the far wall; every single one had to be pre-tuned by tomorrow morning.

Of course, they weren't about to turn me loose with the skis on something as complicated as the WinterSteiger. My job was on the Grindrite, a relatively harmless machine that let me grind the base-high bottoms down to something skiable. Dan walked me through the first pair, his knuckle hovering inches above the belt. Four times through on the shovel, four times on the tail, and then four times all the way through. The only thing you had to look out for was bumping your hip against the red stop button—which I promptly managed to do, sending Tonka, the chocolate lab shop dog, running for cover.

Two-Dog, a 22-year-old, mohawked bump skier who constantly argues with Dan about the best way to bevel, then led me over to the Microwaxer 2000 for another seemingly harmless task. After waxing the other skis in the infirmary, one with a freshly epoxied tip and another with the $40 Deluxe Tune, I called it a night. Hanging up my apron, I joined Dan and Two-Dog for a post-tune beer, booty they received from a friend for mounting a pair of rock skis. Beer and tuning, I found, go together as well.

Lift Op

"Here you go...there you are...here's your chair..." It didn't take long for lift-opping to get monotonous. In fact, just yesterday, Kathleen, a first-year liftie fresh from Chico State, won a bet for spitting out 22 different greetings in a row before repeating herself. "That was pretty hard," she said from the other side of the loading ramp.

Despite the monotony, which last year led to a 120 percent employee turnover rate, lift-opping does have its rewards. Namely, when you sign off for your daily break you have instant access to skiing. And, contrary to what it may look like, it's not just a job for those whose I.Q. matches the number of lift towers. You actually have to be quick on the draw—both for the customers and your cranium. Five minutes into the job, a chair nearly took my head off. "It happens to everyone," said Tim Brunning, 26, a liftie who ended up with four staples in his head from such a collision. "It's moving a lot quicker than you'd think."

To be precise, the Elkhead lift where I was stationed (before it became a high-speed quad) moved at 425 feet per minute, meaning a chair whips around the bullwheel every six seconds. The thing also took 17.5 feet to stop, which doesn't leave you much time to avoid an Interstate-like pile-up. "It's almost impossible to get four people to do four different things at the same time," said Ted Serafy, a 10-year lift op who trained me as if we were about to go into combat. "There's not a lot of time for everyone to get their act together."

In a way, I probably should have been thankful for this. With today's high-speed six-packs you're lucky to have any interaction with riders at all. Even though it wasn't the slapstick action you see in Warren Miller movies, we had plenty. In all, I fetched 11 poles and two skis, and saved three kids teetering on the edge of disaster. With such concentration, it's easy to see why lifties are relieved every 15 minutes. The job is also tough on the body. Grabbing a chair every six seconds spells Advil for sore arms and wrists. It also means you go through gloves quickly. "Three pair a year," said staple-headed Tim. One of mine even caught a ride to Tower 2.

As with any mundane job, you'll get tired of it after a while. But, hey, there's always the shoveling at the end of the day. Even that, however, gets old, and it was easy to see that Rob Jacobs, a 21-year-old from Rochester, New York, was getting a little burned out by the whole lift-op affair. "Don't snowplow next time," he yelled to a skier in a thick New York drawl. "Watch your poles!" In fact, if anyone wanted to bet on it, he probably could have beaten Kathleen's record for greetings.

Burger Flipper

In a way, I'm glad the outside barbecue deck at Rendezvous Lodge was closed when I showed up for my burger-flipping duty: It saved both my schnoz and sunglasses. "You have to wipe the grease off your glasses about 20 times a day," said BBQ supervisor Pete Tufts, whose red hair paled in comparison to his crimson, sunburnt nose. "Plus, the smoke doesn't block the sun too well."

Still, if you can swing it, outside is the place to be—especially come springtime. You're at the controls of a giant party machine, with tunes blaring, people dancing and girls sporting bikinis. Skiing gets set on the back burner as people clog their colons like there's no tomorrow. It's another story if the weather doesn't cooperate. "Sometimes you'll get an inch of snow on top of the burgers," added Pete. And that's why I was ushered inside to join burger-meister Jason Matylewicz, a 21-year-old, first-year flipper with hoops in both ears, and 27-year-old Scott Jauquet, a second-year burger-flipping veteran from Green Bay, Wisconsin.

The first thing I learned is that if you're working inside you don't have to flip. We simply threw patties Frisbee-style into the Nieco Auto Broiler. If you cranked up the speed dial it could handle 200 burgers an hour. The only trick was in the toss; some of the burgers liked to disintegrate mid-air. After feeding the flesh machine I was turned loose at the front counter. "Curly or straight?" I asked the first customer who ordered fries. "Straight," came the reply. "You'll get totally sick of saying that," whispered Jason after I completed the order and figured out that the straight ones have to be loaded in parallel to the rectangular container.

From there, it was on to the grease-splattering machine. Earlier in the year, Scott got splattered in the eye pretty good. And I quickly found that any exposed skin is fair game. "You end up smelling like a burger and fries every day," he said. "That's why you get two uniforms." After dodging onion ring, French fry, and chicken eruptions (the chicken is done when it floats to the top), it was time to take a spell at the set-up counter: lettuce, tomato, onion, pickles, with the top half of the bun face down on the condiments and the bottom half face up next to it. "Only one tomato," chastised Scott after I loaded a plate a mile high with veggies. It's easy to want to play the nice guy and dole out large portions. But in the burger business, you have to stick to your guns, just like the grease sticks to everything from arteries to sunglasses.

Marathon Man

Pat yourself on the back all you want for skiing those 100 days last season. That's peanuts compared to the tally racked up by Rainer Hertrich: He skied—and on teles, no less—2,993 straight days in a row. That's every day for eight years, two months and 10 days.

Hertrich, now 57 and a longtime snow groomer for Copper Mountain, was forced to end his world-record streak in 2011 at his doctor's request only after he was diagnosed with cardiac arrhythmia. Still, against his doctor's advice, he took one last run even that day, bringing his tally just seven days short of a whopping 3,000—every single day since his quirky quest began on Nov. 1, 2003, when the Marlins won the World Series.

Hertrich initiated his Herculean streak after seeing the hoopla around some Jackson Hole skiers who had bragged about notching 6 million vertical feet in a season. After he passed 7 million vertical in 2004, he kept going. And going. And going, through bouts of the flu, such injuries as a separated shoulder and bruised ribs, and weather and logistical hurdles.

Here's how he pulled it off. He tallied six months of daily skiing each year while working at Copper Mountain. Then he'd hit shoulder-season days at Loveland and Arapahoe Basin. From there, he'd continue his streak into each summer as a snowcat driver at Mount Hood in Oregon Then he'd etch the final notches on his ski poles every year by travelling to South America—still somehow managing to eek out runs on consecutive days.

En route, he amassed nearly 100 million vertical feet and a peculiar record in Guinness. Get a life, you might begrudgingly think. Seems to us he's had a great one. Behold a few of his thoughts on his record:

"I don't think I'll ever get too famous from it. But I did end up on CNN once for 17 seconds. They charged me $200 just to get a DVD of it.

"A lot of people say it's inspirational and shows a good work ethic. But I was never looking to give motivational speeches. I'm the one who got to ski.

"To me the vert is more important. That's the record Guinness created: accumulated vertical descent in consecutive days. But skiing a million vertical feet per month is a lot—that's more than Everest, every day.

"You have to remain dedicated. Some days were really tough, and there were a lot of logistics involved. I also skied through some miserable conditions. Minus 20 sometimes. But once I figured out I was on a world record pace it became more of a dedicated project.

"Changing hemispheres was tough. Santiago is three hours later than Timberline. I would pre-pack my gear and take a pre-dawn run on other equipment before my flight. Once I got lost driving in the fog and barely made it in time to put my skins on. Coming home to Colorado, my flight usually arrived in the morning so I'd hit Loveland on the way back.

"You have to ski through pain and illness and just get up and deal. I don't go to doctors. I don't need to know that something hurts. When I separated my shoulder, I still skied the next day; I just didn't plant my pole. I got super sick in Chile for a week, but I skied through it.

"Anything counts, as long as your skis are underfoot on snow. But some days it was just a lone strip somewhere.

"I had sponsors like K2, Volle and Spyder, which helped, but I'd usually spend more than $10,000 or so a year to keep the streak going.

"I think I'm safe with the record. I doubt anyone will ever break it.

Of Brodies and Bridgestone

I'm out of my comfort zone. Not surprising, as I'm about to put the pedal to the metal in a brand new Lexus ES 350 sedan inside, of all places, the Howelsen Ice Arena.

Starting at one blue line, we're supposed to slam on the brakes once we reach the other, at Howelsen a distance of 57 feet, hopefully stopping before we careen into the boards 60 feet later. Rink manager Mike Albrecht stands outside the glass, cringing.

"Make sure you floor it," says my instructor, Robert Ames, as if I was planning on weenieing out.

When the flagman waves, against my better judgment, that's what I do, stomping the gas. The engine roars, tires spin, and we start moving. Well, actually, inching. It's not the breakneck speed I was expecting, but the boards take up more windshield quickly.

We're here burning rink rubber to test Bridgestone's new WS80 Blizzak snow tires. The company has flown in media wonks from around the country—including writers from Road & Track and Car & Driver magazines—to its heralded Bridgestone Winter Driving School to test first-hand the grippiness of its new tires. Hence, the ice rink investigation.

We each get to drive two cars, one with WS80s and the other with competitor Michelin's new X-Ice Xi3s. A third car has WS80s on one side and the Michelins on the other. Step on the brakes and the car turns toward the grippier side.

Earlier, they already had nudged one car up against the boards. I don't want to be victim number two.

I cross the red center ice line where face-offs occur and gain momentum toward the far blue line. "Now!" Ames suggests, imploring me to stomp on the brakes, not a pump, to utilize the ES 350's antilock system.

We glide to a stop, 10 feet from the far boards. I'm in a rig a few thousand pounds heavier than a typical hockey defenseman, but the boards are safe from splintering.

The event has drawn a veritable Who's Who of drivers. At the 8 a.m. product presentation, I stood in the breakfast buffet line next to three-time Indianapolis 500 race car driver Simon Pagenaud. Picking at the food line-up, he compared the croissants to those from his native France. A sniff, a scowl and, finally, a tentative nibble.

At our table, he espoused upon skiing instead of driving. "I love skiing," he said, hinting that he likes it fast. "I ski a lot in the French Alps. I wish I could ski here, but I have another test drive in California."

Surprisingly, he doesn't drive on snow much. "Just for fun sometimes, like here," he said. "But it's great that anyone can access the driving school here and understand what snow driving is all about. It's very different from pavement. It makes you more aware of your environment. It applies to me racing in the Indy and the average person on the road."

That'd be me. I'm comfortable pulling donuts in a parking lot, but beyond that I'm a Sheraton croissant to a French éclair.

Bridgestone marketing exec Phil Pacsi then broke the ice to get the presentation underway.

There are three types of tires, he said—summer, all-season and winter—and at any given time only an area 8.5 by 11 inches touches the ground. That part, then, better stick like Honey Stinger.

In the 1980s, he added, studded snow tires were outlawed in Japan, fueling the Japanese company's development of the studless Blizzak, which hit the U.S. market in 1993. In 2008, Quebec mandated winter tire use, further increasing demand.

That demand has been further fueled by a marketing campaign featuring professional athletes. Stars like Troy Aikman, Deon Sanders, Tim Duncan and soccer's Adam Vinatatte have all been tapped to tout the tires. "The demographics are very close to ours," he continued. "The typical sports fan is our customer."

My eyes then lit upon what looked to be another star spokesman two seats away. He looked different than the typical tire writer—beefier, tougher, more athletic.

This year's Conquer the Cold campaign, it turns out, is being run in partnership with the NHL. The new Blizzaks, Pacsi said, are designed to perform during hockey weather. Last winter, Bridgestone hosted the NHL Winter Classic in front of 105,000 fans outside at the University of Michigan.

Former Colorado Avalanche hockey player Milan Hejduk, who's won the Stanley Cup and two Olympic medals, then took the stage, speaking about his career, Steamboat ("It takes a lot of courage to go off those ski jumps") and tires ("Like hockey skates, you need good traction").

Breakfast and ice-driving accomplished, we pile in a bus and head up to the Bridgestone Winter Driving School off TwentyMile Road. We couldn't have asked for better, or worse, winter driving conditions. Thick fog blanketed everything in sight, from the staging yurt to the tracks. The lighting was as flat as the rink we were just on.

With three separate, two-mile-long tracks, at 77 acres the school is the largest facility of its kind in North America. Directed by Mark Cox, it uses a quarter of a million gallons of water pumped from a nearby pond just to make one of its fish-tailing loops. Entering its 35th year, it employs 10 full-time instructors, including former race car driver Robert Ames. Clients range from regular Joes to military, law and medical personnel—anyone looking to gain an edge driving on snow. During a 95-day season, it will train up to 2,500 snow-leery drivers.

"Two weeks ago we had an ambulance from Grand County that actually had four different tires on it," says an incredulous Ames. "They didn't know any better. Our goal is to help people leave as better drivers and never have to use their deductible."

There are three facets of the Grip Rule, he adds. 1) Your vision—see an opening and have an out; 2) Adjust your speed for the conditions; and 3) The separation of controls, including steering, brake and throttle (brake in a straight line, then release, coast and steer). Other pointers include keeping your hands at 9 and 3 o'clock, and noticing weight transfer (weight shifts to the rear tires as you accelerate, lessening grip for steering; it moves forward as you slow down, offering better steering).

After the whirlwind "Get it? Got it? Good," three of us climb inside a Lexus AWD RX 350 SUV, with Ames riding shotgun. We'll rotate from back to front when it's our turn to drive. I get first dibs. When I hear "All clear!" over the radio from instructor TJ Fry ahead in the lead car, I'm set to go.

It should be called the How to Avoid Understeering School. That's what I do at each turn, as Ames offered pointers. Soon I get the hang of it, the tires biting like Hejduk's hockey blades. It's a far cry from my beater 2001 Explorer.

We take laps on one Lexus with the Blizzaks, another with the Michelins and another with Goodyear UltraGrip Ice WRTs. They're all way better than anything I've ever driven. During one lap, Pagenaud the Indy Racer blasts by and takes out a cone. I slow down to give him some room.

"You can go now," Ames says. "I don't think you'll catch him."

Later we hear the inevitable reprimand over the radio. "We got an extraction," says Fry, pinpointing it between turns six and seven. It's not Pagenaud, but one of us.

"Over-corrected," says Ames. "That's never a good feeling...it means more paperwork."

Instead of soft snow, the banks are ice hard, easily capable of dinging a Lexus. That's why they don't having us goosing it. Instead, they teach us to take it up until the tire's breaking point, just when they start to slide.

But the instructors don't always practice what they preach. At day's end, they disable the cars' traction and stability controls (called "fun switches") and take us around on "hot laps." We spin 180 degrees into turns, then spiral the other way for the next. One instructor does a 270 before correcting. I feel like I'm starring in Starsky and Hutch. "These guys make it look like Simon was taking it easy," says Ames.

At the bar afterward, I clink beers with Pagenaud, who says he could feel a "massive difference" between all three tires. I couldn't really tell; they all seemed sweet.

Later, at dinner, I discover it was Ghandi, the Bridgestone marketer, who had to get "extracted." I also learned that our fabled Indy Car driver accidentally "brushed" a bank. "Just a little," he admits. When a pea falls off Hejduk's plate, he bats it with his knife.

Soon Pacsi arrives with the scores from our ice rink test. My top speed with the WS80s registered 10.3 mph, with a stopping distance of 36 feet. On the Michelins, my high was 9.4 mph with a stopping distance of 45 feet. The Blizzaks registered 18.5 percent better—that much less chance of adding a line item to the rink's maintenance budget.

Then my eyes settle on Indy Boy's score. On my best run, I reached a faster speed than Pagenaud's 10.2 mph. Someone wave the checkered flag.

Ode to the Daffy

It was at an aerials competition here in good ol' Ski Town USA in 1976 that my oldest brother, David, went for an airwalking quadruple daffy, crossed his skis on number three, and woke up in the hospital. Later, we'd know this variation as the "Screamin' Seaman," but it's a mistake you make unintentionally only once.

So why is the daffy—that glorious, crotch-ripping badge of courage involving one or more midair splits—tainted with dorkdom? Pop a daffy under the lift today and you're considered either a hipster or a loser. It's a shame because the daffy is one of skiing's marquee stunts—one that, unlike, say, a cork 540, still is within the grasp of The Everyman Skier.

Its place in the annals of aerials is hallowed, with cameos in everything from "Hot Dog...the Movie" to "Hot Tub Time Machine" and infinite Warren Miller reels. Credit this to its difficulty compared with its more mundane cousins of yesteryear, the twister and spread eagle.

The daffy was how you earned your true stripes on the slopes. It takes guts—and big air—to mock gravity with your tips and tails like that and then get them back underfoot in time to touch down. Lose it on a twister? Who cares? So you land a little sideways. Screw up a daffy and you're exposing your family jewels to the mountain's whim. Of all upright aerials, the daffy places you in the worst crash position imaginable, which is both its bane and its beauty.

"It was definitely the marquee move of its day," says former freestyle competitor, coach and longtime local Park Smalley. "The spread eagle was the easiest, and the daffy came next ... but there was always the fear factor of catching that tip."

In typical one-upsmanship, people couldn't get enough of a good thing and soon began linking the signature move. Smalley says aerialist Chris "Fuzz" Feddersen once linked five of them together, each one extending past the 180-degree, groin-pulling split mark. "Fuzz had the best daffies of anyone," says local Olympian Nelson Carmichael, who won the bronze in the bumps at the 1992 Winter Games and used to sport a mean daffy himself. "Daffies were iconic because the good ones looked great from any angle. They felt great, too, seeing how far you could stretch, using your skis' momentum to swing your feet."

As for my own brush with the leg stretching and tip-catching badge of courage, my worst performance came on a simple double-daffy attempt on the back side of Lake Eldora. One stride, two strides, a cross and a bone-rattling crunch. It psyched me out for years, relegating me to lamer splitsters—a weak alternative with the splits, and tips, off to the side—for the duration of my daffy career.

You also could catch your tips on other things. Smalley remembers a Tequila Cup event in the '70s when he hit a jump, threw a daffy and accidentally soared in his splits over the perimeter fence and out of the course. "It got high points," he says.

Do it right, however, and it's pure Picasso. Nowhere is this illustrated better than on a black-and-white poster hanging in my mom's living room in Boulder, showing my other brother, Stephen, throwing a heroic daffy off a homemade kicker in Chautauqua Park, the Third Flatiron framed perfectly between his outstretched, Nadia Comaneci legs. For me, the younger brother still melting together my older siblings' used P-Tex sticks, that represented skiing at its finest. He even added the words "Ski Boulder" below it, Lange-poster style (speaking of which, it's also a move where you follow their bosomed model's advice to "Keep those tips up").

The irony is that the move disappeared just as skis began getting shorter, which actually makes daffies easier than they were when we boosted them on tip-grabbing 205s.

So to all you closet daffy-throwers out there now skiing on fatter, shorter skis, let's resurrect this classic airborne spacewalk. Let's raise our glasses and throw back a beer to raising our tails and throwing back our tips. Pick a catwalk, mogul or other lip, throw one foot forward and the other back, and moonwalk Mount Werner, unleashing a move that, for too long, has been nudged backstage by mute grabs, corks and rodeos.

Think globally, daffy locally.

Powder Mode

It's hard after nine months to get back into the powder swing—especially on a bad snow year when the first one doesn't come until January. There are a lot of things to remember and nary time to spare. And despite all your best-laid plans, sometimes fate causes inevitable delays.

While there might not be pressure to perform on hardpack, that changes when the high pressure system leaves and is replaced by the year's first powder storm. You have to be on it, your synapses firing as fast as the falling snowflakes.

For those juggling jobs and kids, the preparation starts the day before. First, check your work calendar. Oops, a meeting at 10 a.m. Time to reschedule. Next, pitch in with the kid shuttles; you'll work late the next day and won't be able to help. This means less heat on the homefront.

Next on the list: a pre-emptive snowblow of the driveway. Hopefully, it fires up on the first pull, unless you forgot to drain the gas in the spring. And don't forget to aim the chute away from the shed door, splattering everything inside.

Then comes the shoveling. Dang, the shovel still is at the Nordic center, where you volunteered last weekend. No matter. Neighbor Dave provides a loaner that lets you do the minimum, shoveling off the front steps, back porch and trampoline, which is somehow still up.

Time to think more ahead. You make a lunch so you can eat at your desk the next day, pack a set of clothes to change into back at the office, and lay your ski clothes out so dressing doesn't cut into the morning's kid-readying time.

But wait, there's still more to do, helping with dishes, piano practice and homework, all in the name of wracking up spousal points. Only then do you pull out your fat skis for the first time of the year and load them atop the car. One less thing to remember in the morning. For them, it's go time. No more letting your rock skis get all the action.

As expected, you hear the plows outside in the morning. You dial the snow report—cold, but 11 inches at mid-mountain. You help the kids with their Cheerios, peel a kiwi, and usher their lunch boxes into their backpacks. All that's left is dropping them off at school.

But then comes "The Berm." You haven't had to battle it yet this winter. The shoveling costs you a good 40 turns on the mountain.

Backing out, you close the garage door only to see it stop halfway down. You push the remote again and it goes back up. Up, down, up, down. Finally, you run inside to close it manually. Another 30 turns lost.

Oops. You forgot your daughter's violin inside. That'll cost you another 20 turns.

By the time you reach school, the car's thermometer reads 15 below zero. You walk your daughter into school but forget her art project in the car. Another 25 turns lost—and that's if you hustle. Then you narrowly miss the yellow light on Lincoln Avenue. Your chances at untracked are unraveling.

Decision time. Where to park? T-bar? Not worth the 10 bucks. Ski Town Square? Full by now. Knoll Lot? Probably full as well, and who knows if that music tent still is up. You settle for Meadows, parking five rows back.

Then your fortunes change—the shuttle is there waiting. The frenzy inside is palpable, a season's worth of pent-up powder demand about to be unleashed. People file out quickly, like shoppers hitting Macy's on Black Friday. You do the same, but there's a glitch. Your skis fell off the rack. If you were counting missed turns before, now it's entire runs. The drivers eventually find them on their next round, but you've fumbled the ball at the goal line.

The good news is that now the gondo line is empty, the glass-pressers long since gone. Decision time again: Which run? A number of factors come into play, from crowds to the hour to what's lurking beneath. You opt for Whiteout, which proves a good choice. Skier's left still is relatively unscathed.

The Storm Peak Express maze is full, like fans lining up for a Phish concert. You blow it by not going to the far side. Up top you face another crucial decision. You opt for another old faithful, Closets, aware of the shallow base. Soon, you're floating through turns instead of hearing them, all that effort to get here finally paying off. And you have the first powder day of the season under your belt, so you'll be that much better prepared next time.

Readying for Old Man Winter

While skiers annually flock to the Steamboat Springs Winter Sports Club's ski swap to pick through everyone else's rejects to upgrade their own quivers, for me it's another gear exchange that truly marks the change of the seasons. Only this one involves the garage rather than the school gymnasium.

The ritual is always the same. Move everything from its summer berth—the kayaks, rafts, bikes, pogo sticks, tents, backpacks, fishing gear, coolers and more—back into its crawlspace nooks to make room for cars and ski gear. It also involves digging through the crawlspace for the duct tape-labeled trash bags full of winter apparel stashed away all summer. All that gets shuttled up to the mudroom, where, unwashed from last year, it assumes its respective hooks. Then you recycle those same trash bags by filling them anew with flip-flops, sandals, rain jackets, umbrellas and other fair-weather fare to shuttle back down.

This annual Changing of the Gear Guard is just the price of admission for living in a ski town. It comes without fanfare and is a formality everyone here has to do.

Like leaves turning color from decreasing chlorophyll, a few key indicators from Mother Nature usually trigger the response. The onset of football season and surprise darkness of Daylight Savings Time are the earliest harbingers, followed by the year's first frost, requiring you to scrape your car windows bare-handed with a CD case (since you can't find your real scraper). Then come the actual snowstorms. Procrastinate too long and your lawn flamingos will be buried until spring.

The Great Garage Shuffle precipitates other seasonal transitions as well. You swap out swim goggles for ski goggles in mudroom cubbies; replace bike socks in your sock drawer for longer, ski-oriented ones; and move snow shovels and sleds to their posts on the porch. Hula Hoops, scooters and soccer balls have to be swept clean from the yard; the sprinkler-blow-out guy needs a reminder call; garden hoses need to get detached; the lawnmower gets replaced by the snowblower in the shed; the trampoline has to be taken down, including pads and skin-pinching springs; and the outside furniture needs to get shuttled from avalanche zones to the house's south side.

Then come the errands. Foremost, the car tires need to be changed, hopefully before that jaunt to the Front Range. You also have to visit the rental store to outfit the kids with gear. Let's see...lease or buy? Maybe both, since they'll need Alpine, nordic, tele and snowboard. Add a woodstove to the mix and the laundry list grows longer still. And none of this considers waxing and tuning snowboards and skis, sewing that duct-taped hole in your ski pants, or fixing that broken pole basket, all tasks you swore you'd do last year.

So contrary to what Front Rangers and other visitors might think, life here isn't all powder days, pub crawls and jacuzzis. Come winter, these tasks and more rear their ugly heads as part of the transition to Ski Town USA. But take it in stride; it's all just part of surviving the seasons. And if you're like me and overlook a few things—like hosing off your mountain bike after the weekend's final muddy ride—don't worry...it's nothing the first powder day won't help you forget.

A Ride with Ray

I might as well have been riding with Jerimiah Johnson.

If ever there was a stand-in for the famed mountain man, who actually trapped just north of here, it's fourth-generation Steamboat local Ray Heid, who runs Del's Triangle 3 Ranch outside Clark.

I'm here with my daughter, Casey, for our first-ever winter horseback ride. Ray, saddling horses in a hand-sewn knee-length elk skin coat with beaver pelt collar, is our guide. Topping its furry collar are a balaclava and cowboy hat to ward off cold that cripples us but doesn't phase Ray. A cocoon of cheeks, nose and eyes is all we can see.

At 80, he's still as active as ever, as evidenced by three sets of perfect figure-eight ski tracks etched into the hillside above the horse corral. They're as obvious as they are aesthetic, and he's as proud of them as he is his ranching operation, which he's been running since 1985.

Hopping on his saddle, he says they now do about as many guests in the winter as they do in the summer. It's easy to see why as soon as our horses— Casey's docile mare named Tia and mine a gelding named Bodie—step out of the corral and into the surrounding wonderland. There's not a whisper of wind; all is tranquil, silent and white. It's as peaceful a setting as you could script. Weasel tracks pitter-patter this way and that, snowy cottonballs cling to scrub oak, and a piercing blue sky whitens the winter white.

It doesn't take long for Ray to interrupt the serenity. The plod of his horse, Stormy, kicks his story synapses into gear. "One year, we named all the horses by the weather," he begins. "Stormy, Breezy, Windy, Sunny and Chinook. Another year we named them all after spices." Behind us, other guests straddle Cinnamon, Wasabi and Ginger.

If his horses are an integral part of his ranch and ski lifestyle, so is his family. His mother, Ruby, was the sister of Steamboat icon Hazie Werner. Brother Corkey qualified for the 1956 Cortina Olympics and headed the

Steamboat ski patrol, while brother Del ran the resort's lift department. His son Rowan ("Perk") works on the ranch, as does Perk's wife, Becky, and grand kids Justin and Jason, making six generations of Heids leaving their mark in Ski Town, USA. While Ray can't put his finger on how many horses they have, or how many guests they take riding each year, it's a lot. Today there are 13 of us, most visitors taking a break from Steamboat's slopes. He's out there with them most every day, rain, show or shine. "We had to cancel our first trip in years earlier this week," he says as we saunter up the hill, our horses' breath the only wisps of clouds in the sky. "It was 27 below. We'll go out in pretty much anything."

Eventually, his tales turn to his other love, skiing. He's been at it 77 years, since leather straps served as bindings. This year he wants to ski 80 days to match his age. He also monitors the inches of fresh snow he skis. Every time he tracks up a new storm, it adds to the tally. So far he's over 150 fresh inches for the year.

It helps that he finally gave up his teles for a pair of AT bindings. No longer can pal Billy Kidd, his nemesis at CU while he was coaching at Wyoming, joke about him "not being able to afford the other "heel" half of his binding."

Most of Ray's stories center around skiing or riding, or some whacko combination thereof. (He says he'd "hate to ever have to choose between the two.") Like how he first donned skis at age 3 to ride the boat tow up Howelsen Hill; how he'd ski from his uncle's ranch down to Twentymile Road to catch a ride into town; how he grew up skiing with his cousins the Werners; and how he became a four-way skier in downhill, slalom, jumping and cross country for the University of Wyoming before making the 1960 Olympic ski jumping team. Or how he ran New Mexico's Sierra Blanca ski area before returning to Steamboat to run the ranch in 1985.

The combo tales would hold court at any saloon, especially those revolving around horsebacking up to ski Sand Mountain every spring. One time a freak lightning storm chased them off. "There were five flashes before I could even count to one," he says, the memories coming as easily as his sway in the saddle. "My theory is that you're better off staying on your horse— they're always lifting two feet so you have less contact with the ground."

Or the time Warren Miller visited to film horses galloping through the snow, only to have Ray's ride stumble and somersault, catapulting Ray through the air. "What do you make of that?" he asks. "He's the best ski filmmaker in the world and he didn't even get the shot."

As we crest an aspen-filled ridge and see the snow-clad Zirkel range come into view, his stories take a turn to the olden days—of how his grandmother rode 70 miles in a blizzard from Wolcott to Stagecoach to tend to a sick child, or the Frenchman he met in Brown's Park who holds the Guinness Record for longest horse ride, from the Straits of Magellan to Fairbanks, Alaska. He still gets cards from him every year.

Before we begin our loop back, he hops off his saddle like someone a third his age, landing in a two-foot-deep snowbank. He then postholes down the line checking guests' saddles. Returning, he stretches his leg up into the stirrup and pulls himself back in the saddle. "Sometimes it's tough because the horse is a few feet higher up on the packed trail and you're down in the powder," he says.

With that he's back on, leading both the conversation and equines behind him. Soon we make our way off the ranch's 260 acres and onto BLM land. "You can ride from here all the way to Wyoming, all on public land," he says. "Not a bad backyard."

Indeed, if he had his druthers, which he usually does, he'd ride every day—which is what helped him get voted town's Best Cowboy. "I ride for a living six days a week, ride for fun on Sundays, and then, for vacation, go somewhere else to ride," he says. And he loves sharing it with others. "I love watching people evolve to love it," he says. "You get out there and hear nothing but the horses' hoofs and breathing and the wildlife calling, and you think, 'this is the way to live.'"

He still rides a custom saddle, copied from his grandmother's, that he had built for him in 1993 by former Saddle Maker of the Year Pete Correll. He figures he has more than 36,000 miles on it, riding an average of four hours per day, six days a week for 25 years.

At a downed log harboring a two-foot-high stripe of powder, he's off his mount again, this time post-holing through the snow with horse in tow, packing out the route. It's a chore he's accustomed to. Often he'll go out on solo rides to pack the trail, prodding ahead with a ski pole to find the wind-blown way.

Soon, his figure-eight ribbons above the corral come into view again, basking in the alpenglow as the sun nudges the far ridge. It's as if he timed it this way, the orange aura highlighting their every curve. As he hops off Stormy and helps guests out of their saddles, I can't help but think perhaps he was born a century too late. But then he wouldn't have those Dynafits to reach his 80 ski days.

Riding Rasmussen-style

My helmet didn't exactly paint me with experience. It was bright yellow, with two giant, dorkily grinning smiley faces adorning each side. Jason, at Steamboat Powersports, loaned it to me to join my buddy Edge in an off-piste snowmobile lesson from pro rider Brett Rasmussen. The helmet didn't reek of skill or sponsorship.

A diehard backcountry skier, Edge, vice-president of avalanche gear company Backcountry Access, was hitting Rabbit Ears to learn riding tips from one of its sponsored athletes, Rasmussen. If he's selling backcountry safety gear to the snowmobile market, including avi beacons, airbags, protective apparel and more, he might as well walk the fossil fuel-burning walk. Did I want to tag along?

Hasta luego office and hello indoctrination to off-piste riding—and digging.

To set the stage, I'm not much of a powersports guy. This was pure baptism by fire. I grew up in the tofu and telemark town of Boulder, where you burn more patchouli oil than fossil fuel. We wear Birkenstocks instead of snowmobile boots, and earn our turns instead of burn them.

Sure, I've snowmo-skied Buff Pass like any resident worth his or her polypro. But this has always been on packed roads where you simply sit and steer. Do that off-piste and you'll have as much direction as a typical ski bum.

Smiley helmet in hand, I met them at the East Summit, next to a giant trailer with a "Ride Rasmussen Style" logo painted on the side. A thin 57-year-old, Rasmussen didn't look the part of a snowmobiling icon. Nor did his fellow instructor and cousin Bryan Bennett. But they're snowmo studmos.

Rasmussen co-founded and competed on the Rocky Mountain Snowmobile Hillclimb Association series for 15 years, one of the sport's most prestigious events (one race used to be held in Meeker). A six-time world champion, he now teaches off-piste riding clinics from Siberia and Iceland to Sweden and Norway.

His Ski-doo sponsored sled attests to his snowmobile stripes: It's a 164-horse, direct-injection, two-stroke Summit XM, with three-inch track lugs and a 174-inch track length, the tallest and longest ever made. It equals one suped-up package, as long as you have the skill to ride it. Which is what we were here to learn.

After introductions, we fired up our sleds and crossed the highway, where a b-b-bumpy road took us to a perch above an untracked hill. Here, Rasmussen offered a quick introduction, outlining the four main riding positions—from neutral (standing, while straddling the seat) to hanging your weight off the edge like hiking out on a sailboat. The positions are used to tilt the machine on edge to turn it. Combine this weight transfer with counter-steering and a liberal dose of throttle and cajones and you're off and running.

If only it were that easy.

With this "Get it, got it, good" crash course, he took off across the slope, arcing his sled on edge and cranking a beautiful turn back uphill. Now it was our turn. Like ducklings, we flailed and wallowed in his wake. None of us could keep his line and instead bailed downhill. Had it been above a cliff, we'd all be toast.

There are two problems: 1) the whole turning-the-opposite-way thing is counterintuitive; and 2) you're juggling a lot of balls. It's like chewing gum, patting your head and rubbing your belly, all while wrestling a 500-lb. machine. You have to give it juice, hang off the side and put it on edge, and then steer it the opposite way every survival gene in your body tells you to. While he likened it to riding a bike, our only training wheels are the trees whizzing by.

A little too late, he also stressed the importance of saving energy, both in handling the machine and planning ahead so you don't get stuck. But we were already in grovel-ville, rookie golfers leaving divots wherever we went. While Rasmussen made it look effortless, I would have had more luck wrestling a rhino. After one particularly deep auger, I was too pooped to even pull my starter cord.

But then, in one magic moment, you feel it. You discover that counter-steering actually does help balance the thing when it's up on edge. And you take off on a graceful, arcing turn, blending a perfect combination of power and balance. No matter that this takes you right into a tree well, causing you to shed your last semblance of dignity and call in the cavalry. For a moment, you felt it.

Umpteen Rasmussen-rescues later, we regrouped after Etch-a-Sketching a hill into a line painting. I had rolled mine, toppled mine, buried mine and even rode it switch back downhill after botching a hill climb. But he bailed me out every time, a guardian angel goosing the throttle.

We all illustrated a few common mistakes, he advised, including not committing to the edge or counter-steer. It came down to not trusting the technique. Indeed, I had moments of brilliance, followed by spastic sessions when I couldn't turn it for the life of me. During such mental blocks, the advantage went to the machine.

But by the time we made it back to the trailer, fully appreciating the packed-out road home, I came away with a new appreciation for the sport and Steamboat's stature in it. It's not so bad, I felt, having long-dead organisms provide the power in snow country. And contrary to what neophytes might think, it isn't for Bugles-eating couch potatoes, even if that's what Bryan pulled out at lunch.

It's another incredible reason to live in an area covered by snow half the year—despite tweaking muscles you never knew you had. And most importantly? Afterward, my own grin matched my helmet's smiley faces.

The Scarlet Letters

Live in mountain towns long enough and there's a good chance it'll happen, the bane of all skiers and bikers. "Can't tell for sure without an MRI," said Dr. Bryan Bomberg, "but 70 percent chance it's your ACL."

The words sunk in like a skinny ski in spring glop. I might as well have been told I had the plague. Thirty-eight years skiing and the scarlet letters had finally surfaced. The rest of my ski season, including a high school reunion trip to the Selkirks, disappeared in the snap of a ligament.

I'd made it to the end of the halfpipe, throwing 360s on each hit. Each time I caught enough air to glance around at the 90-meter jump and ball fields abutting Howelsen Hill downtown. One more and it'd be back to work after another classic Steamboat lunch break. But I got greedy. On the last hit, thinking I was 20 years younger, I went for a grab halfway through my rotation, overshooting it by a goatee hair—just enough to land in the transition zone, and transition my season into rehab.

My knees weren't immaculate to begin with—my left one was scoped after four years of college lacrosse, and my right knee met rock telemarking on a backcountry trip. But neither injury involved ligaments, nor made me second-guess my recreational future. I'd competed in bumps, skied fourteeners, worked ski patrol, played hockey and lived in ski towns from Telluride to Steamboat for years with nary a problem. I was beginning to feel immune to the malady.

But harbingers had already reared their heads. It was already a bad year for ACLs. Each time the phone rang, it seemed, I learned of another friend suffering the plight. My friend Edge blew his playing hockey on the Front Range; Dan tore his playing soccer; and Bruce fell victim to a fluke backcountry turn in Telluride. Each call made me cringe.

Though the prestigious Steadman-Hawkins clinic was just two hours away in Vail, without the pocketbook of Terrel Davis or Picabo

Street I went to Bomberg, a kayaking friend who had treated my earlier backcountry bang-up. Though he once traded a patient cortisone shots for a kayak, I wasn't trying for a pro form; I was paying full retail, hoping to get back on my feet as soon as possible.

But for now, I was relegated to the sidelines. The morning before my MRI, I hobbled to the finish line of the local winter Penthalon. I was supposed to compete, but tried to look on the bright side; maybe it saved me from having a heart attack. Then other like-kneed sorts started tracking me down.

"What happened?" asked a man noticing my limp. "ACL," I replied, pointing to the halfpipe responsible. Turns out he had gotten his cut four weeks earlier. Like a scene from Invasion of the Body Snatchers, I then ran into five other locals with rebuilt ACLs—inside people who looked perfectly normal on the outside. We seemed to gravitate to each other, as if to share in our respective afflictions. People who I'd otherwise never even talk to suddenly became friends in commiseration. It was a club with the camaraderie of AA, with survivors quick to lend support.

According to Steadman-Hawkins, more than 200,000 ACL surgeries are performed in the U.S. each year. Such wasn't the case in the early days. It was France's Amédée Bonnet who first described an ACL rupture's three essential signs in 1845: "A snapping noise, haemarthrosis and loss of function are characteristic of ligamentous injury in the knee," he wrote. I remembered hearing a Rice Krispies-like "pop!" on my landing.

In 1880 it was Greece's Georges Noulis who described the ACL's role and how to test its strength, a technique known as today's Lachman test. Dr. Bomberg employed it on mine. Grabbing my swollen excuse for a knee, now puffed up like a hot air balloon, he pulled my tibia forward. Then he grimaced. Not a good sign. It stayed there instead of snapping back. He might as well have tattooed the three letters onto my forehead.

The first ACL repair came in 1895 when A.W. Mayo Robson stitched together two torn ligaments on a 41-year-old miner injured in an earth fall. Six years later the miner described his knee as "perfectly strong." Replacement attempts didn't fare as well. The first came in 1903, using braided silk. It didn't work. Neither did using silver wire 15 years later. Things picked up with Dacron and carbon fiber replacements in the '70s, but results were still poor (carbon deposits were later found on some patients' livers). Then came Gore-tex and today's best options: your hamstring, patellar tendon or cadaver. Bacon, kneecap or corpse.

Bomberg recommended the bacon.

The MRI machine at the Yampa Valley Medical Center buzzed and zapped, rearranging the hydrogen atoms in my leg as I lay in a tube up to my neck, staring at a giant General Electric logo. Mick Jagger (whose lips might make a decent ligament) played into earphones, but it couldn't drown out the sound of my atoms realigning. Soon the attendant came back into the room.

"That's it," he said. "We'll send the results to your doctor's office." The next day's visit confirmed it. "That's where it should be," said Dr. Doom. "Right where those gray shards are."

While the cross-section of my patellar tendon stood out like a tree stump, my ACL was obliterated. Then he explained my options. I could forego the surgery, but I'd likely always have a trick knee that could cause more damage; or I could simply watch a piece off my hamstring miraculously transform into a new ACL.

The details made me queasy. "It's really quite routine," he said. "We just drill a hole into the femur and tibia and screw in screws which..." I tried to cut him off. "And while we're in there," he continued, "we might as well work on that kneecap of yours." He sounded like my mechanic, who fixed my water pump while replacing the timing belt. The theory: While they're under the hood, also micro-fracture the backside of the kneecap to encourage cartilage growth.

Word got out about my predicament. Friends harassed me about missing the Selkirk trip. Others made me question the surgery altogether. "I haven't had an ACL since '83," said my cousin Homer, a telemarker and World Cup C-1 paddler—a sport requiring kneeling in cold water. "I haven't had one for seven years," added Fritz, a friend whose soccer and hockey teams always beat ours. That neither of them had insurance at the time seemed moot; they seemed to be doing just fine.

After a week or so my knee was starting to feel better—especially after the doc drained a few Budweisers of fluid from it. "That's how you want it when you go in for surgery," he said. "You want to feel like, 'What the heck am I going in for?'"

I scheduled surgery for a week later: Thursday, March 22, at a festive 4:20 p.m. I could have delayed it a week, but then it would have fallen on my birthday—and I didn't think I'd be in the mood to blow out candles.

The days leading up to it were filled with anxiety I hadn't experienced since my college thesis. I tossed and turned in bed, one dream slating me for chemotherapy right before knee surgery. Reality wasn't much better:

a powder day came and I was the only one at the office; a friend's band played and I was the only wallflower.

I prepared for ACL D-Day as best I could, knowing I'd soon be immobile. I moved the snowblower to its summer abode, turned the futon back into a couch, and re-shuffled the recycle containers to their spring location. My ski gear got put away without fanfare in its mid-season state: goggles remained cracked, skis unwaxed, and a tail clip still missing from a climbing skin.

My last memory before they rolled me away is of the nurse scribbling "No!" on my good knee. How thoughtful. Maybe they should write the same thing on my gall bladder.

When I awoke, I promptly puked on the nurses, a thank-you chunder from being put under. They were as glad to get rid of me as I was of my innards, and my wife drove me home in my drugged-up stupor. The next three days passed in a fog of oxycodone (one to two tablets every four hours); toradol/ketorolac (one four times a day as needed for pain); oxycontin (one twice daily for long-acting pain); plus promethazine to combat it all (one every six hours as needed for nausea).

Friends came and went in a blur. Pete came with PlayStation and 13 game CDs, followed by Joe with a six-pack and guitar book. I appreciated the visits, but could see the rationale behind visiting hours. Some had ulterior motives; with the visits came the mysterious disappearance of my gear. "Sorry about your knee," they'd say. "Hey, can I borrow your snowboard?"

A typical day saw me go from bed to couch and, 148 channels later, back again. I learned all the tricks of slouchdom. The couch became my locker, dining, rec, study and TV room, not necessarily in that order. Balancing frozen peas and corn on top of my knee, I became TV Boy, watching Agassi defeat Rafter in the Ericsson Open, Woods take the Players Championships, and Arizona topple Illinois in the NCAA Round of Eight. I read a bio of the Grateful Dead, which made me feel better about having a beer with my medication. Slouching became an art form, everything kept within reach of something else. I'd use my crutch to reach sweat pants on the floor, the phone antennae to roll an orange across the coffee table.

All this slouching, of course, was just downtime from rehab: four sets a day of quad and hamstring flexes, leg raises and excruciating towel-induced knee bends. I'd do one set before getting out of bed just to get it out of the way. Like building a house, you had your big show days and your not-so-big-show days. Some days you're sanding drywall, seeing no appreciable gains, and the next you're framing walls, your knee bending to 90 degrees. My biggest came day five, when the doc said I could replace the Toradol with Ibuprofen and Percocet. No more Grateful Dead drug funk. "Take Ibuprofen during the day, and then reward yourself with a little Percocet cocktail at night," he said.

Once off the hard stuff, pain entered the picture. When standing, gravity sucked the swelling down like a snow slough. Percocet cocktail time. I also had to adapt to crutches. Efficiency of motion was key. Never go anywhere without carrying something: Grabbing a pencil with your pinky might save an entire trip later. Apart from the vacant crutch-under-each-arm refrigerator stare, the only way to eat was to play leap frog by resting a plate on barstool, crutching, and then pulling the whole plate-topped tower over.

Rehab efficiency was also important: I'd do leg lifts while stirring oatmeal, knee bends while bathing my daughter, and chair squats while reading the paper. I'd also babysit for friends, figuring to cash in the recreation points later. It was also a good time to have the in-laws visit.

The days went by. As the swelling subsided and atrophy set in, the brace straps had to be tightened. With the micro-fractures, my recovery was harder than most ACL-only repairs. It meant I had to lock my brace straight for four weeks whenever I weighted it. At 10 days, I got rid of a crutch and went back to work, converting the office into a makeshift physical therapy ward. The roller chair serviced hamstring pulls and the desktop facilitated leg curls.

The physical therapist clinic, of course, worked better. And the three-day-a-week visits were also a welcome social affair, with the same people cheering each other on. Warren was in for shoulder surgery from a double-ejecting pile-drive. Steve was in for pre-surgery rehab, slated for ACL replacement a week later, three weeks before his wife was due with their first baby. Terrain Park Victim Pat did his second ACL two weeks earlier. You could compare progress, relishing your victories and bemoaning setbacks.

"Every knee is different," admonished Nikki, my physical therapist, when I'd question someone else's success. A Whine List posted by the door recorded tantrums for all to see.

At two weeks the bike pedals went all the way around, more by accident than perseverance. I whined and made the board. Week four saw the most tangible results. I drove for the first time and took my first braceless steps. This also meant forsaking the sweat pants and rejoining the fashion-conscious. It took a while to eliminate the limp, and Nikki scowled every time I crossed the parking lot. I walked around saying "heel, toe" to ensure proper extension.

At six weeks I realized that life isn't over with a few scarlet letters. (My physical therapist's husband said tearing his was life altering—he started managing a physical therapist business, met his wife and generally got his act together.) And, if anything, it's made me appreciate my knee's years of faithful, flat-landing service. I missed a cat-skiing trip, but my timing could have been worse. It was the end of March. A month more of rehab and I might be able to kayak, where you don't need knees anyway. Two months more and it would be mountain bike season, which would strengthen me for ski season again. And it gave me something a little deeper to write about than the powder I missed in the Selkirks.

A week after surgery, I called my friend John to see how the Selkirk trip went. "How was it?" I asked. A pause filled the line. "Good," he said. "We got two feet while we were up there."

He didn't sound overly ecstatic. Another pause. "But I'm in your boat now," he continued, foreshadowing an ironic twist of ligaments and fate. "I did my ACL on the first day." The scarlet letters had finally paid him a visit, too.

Skiing for Tree Porn

I'm skiing through a grove of aspen trees high on Buffalo Pass, a spring warm spell texturing the snow a cross between powder and corn. The combo seems oddly fitting, as I'm searching for a phonetic cross between the two as well: porn. More specifically, hidden stashes of erotic tree art etched into area's aspens by long lost—and obviously lonely—sheepherders.

We know they're around here somewhere. Guide friends at Steamboat Powdercats had told us about a particular cluster, and we're here to see them for our own perverted selves. "They're a little harder to find than some of the others," they advised. "They're also a little more hard core, so we don't always take our clients there."

That was all we needed to hitch a ride on a snowmobile, skin up a ridge and begin our quest. Ski powder for erotic tree art…who wouldn't buckle up for that?

"That looks like it," said my friend Dave, veering left into a grove of aspens.

We stop in a cluster of trees and glance around. At first all we see sticking out of the virgin snow are the blank, white trunks of thick aspen.

Then our eyes discern something markedly man made—and less virginal. There, on a particularly consistent trunk is a sultry looking masterpiece: a voluptuous and obviously well-endowed naked woman, complete with a knot serving as a navel.

The curves of her hips follow the pattern of our ski tracks: simple, suggestive and smooth. One elbow is cocked in the air in a "Come hither, big boy" pose, her hand disappearing into a crop of Betty Rubble hair. The other elbow forms an erotic arc next to her hip, her hand resting provocatively on her derriere. The breasts aren't abrasive or even obnoxious. They look as if they belong on the drawing every bit as much as the bark belongs on the tree.

It's Marilyn and Zsa Zsa rolled into one is-it-hot-in-here package. Since the lovestruck sheepherder carved it during summer grazing season, winter's high heels have elevated our vantage so my eyes are now above her torso.

While this particular carving is well off the beaten path, there are easier places to carve turns to view tree carvings. But as with love, they're often subject to the winds of change. One such spot was a popular Powdercats drop-off point called Naked Lady Tree, which showed another buxomed beauty baring all to skiersby. But the tree fell down, carrying with it the carver's heartfelt dreams and desires.

Indeed, unlike your typical Van Gogh, the amorous artwork has a limited lifespan. The average aspen lives 100 years, tops. With the region's etchings appearing in earnest in the early 1920s, many of the drawings' days are numbered.

Which is a shame for us voyeuristic skiers. "Erotica is definitely the predominant theme of most of the area's aspen tree carvings," said Angie KenCarin, former district archaeologist for the Medicine Bow-Routt National Forest who recorded the art for more than 15 years. "There are some Spanish narratives and religious drawings, but most of it is pretty sexual. I think these guys were pretty lonely.

"They were bored with nothing to do," she added. "But what do you expect—they sit with sheep all day."

Anything 50 years or older on federal lands has to be recorded, so scouring the countryside for erotic art used to be all in a day's work for KenCarin. Earlier, I sat in her office sifting through hundreds of digital photos she had recorded of area tree art. Pictures of snakes, a Charlie Brown-looking kid and a giant mosquito pixeled to life, as did an etching from California Park with the words Primero and Segundo and a marking from ETA, a Basque underground movement.

All of them provide a window into the past. "The dates are great for us," she said. "A bunch are from the same timeframe in the 1920s when we had a big influx of sheep grazing from the north along the Wyoming Trail. Cataloging the art helps us mark the old stock driveway corridors."

The art, she added, also depicts things that were bothering the carvers. Written in Spanish, one reads, "You couldn't pay me $1 million dollars to come back here." Another Spanish entry reads, "It is so sad to be alone." But women, in varying states of undress, are the clear front runners.

"Carving on trees was an easy way for them to express their feelings," she said. "And aspens are the natural outlet—their bark makes a great canvas." While she admitted that today's sheepherders "aren't doing it to the extent they used to—you don't see very much new stuff," the etchings are predominant enough that local landowner Limon Orton once pursued securing a grant to produce photos of them. KenCarin and the late local photographer Jupiter Jones also contemplated an Arbor Erotica coffee table book highlighting local hotspots, including one near Hahn's Peak harboring a patch dubbed Porno Alley (Jones had compiled a vast photo collection of the art). The annual Wooden Ski Rendezvous at Columbine Cabins often organizes a ski tour there.

"They're all over the place," said Jones, before he passed away in 2016. "You can find them about anywhere sheep would go. Many are on vantage points, carved as they moved around to different grazing grounds." And many, he added, seem to have been drawn by the same person. "Whoever he was," Jones said, "he was a very talented artist."

Whether the bosomed etching before us on Buff Pass belongs to this same artist or not, its voluptuous curves eventually encourage us to continue making our own tracks through the snow. Averting our eyes, we tour out of the aspen grove into an open meadow and make a series of sensuous arcs down to the valley floor. After all, skier or artist, there's nothing better than leaving your mark on virgin terrain.

Skiing with STARS

Forget the local fundraiser Dancing with the Stars...I'll take skiing for STARS.

That's the take-home from joining a team on the annual STARS Challenge, a ski-around-the-mountain event benefitting Steamboat Adaptive Recreational Sports.

"It's one of our top fundraisers of the year," says event director Todd Gollnick, adding that last year's event raised $70,000 for the organization. "And all proceeds go to helping build our programming for people with disabilities."

With participants committed to raising $250, the event kicked off at the Steamboat Grand with a martini-fueled party where participants found out their teams, mingled with Olympians, met their mountain guides and picked up their bibs (I was given No. 69, go figure). I was assigned to the presenting sponsor Yampa Valley Bank team, led by bank president P.J. Wharton, with our token Olympian none other than Nelson Carmichael, giving us an edge in air, flair and hair.

The real action began Saturday morning, where teams gathered at the gondola base, got a quick rundown from Gollnick, and then rode to the top of Thunderhead to begin their quest, which included riding all of Steamboat Ski Area's lifts and visiting key landmarks en route. You earned points by visiting certain areas, all tracked by FLAIK tracking devices worn around team leaders' ankles, as if they were on probation.

After a group photo, like the Rope Drop of yesteryear everyone was off, some clearly more organized about their route than others. While some teams had it all mapped out, we were a bit more improvisational. After some back and forth, we went down a boilerplate Vagabond, posed for a group photo at the teepee, and rode the Thunderhead lift, knocking three must-haves off our list.

On our second run, we got more strategic, or so we thought. We arrived at Storm Peak Express before it opened, losing time. Oops. On the plus side, it allowed the snow to soften a smidgen. We made up for it with our next combo: pole-clinking the Buddy Werner statue, skiing Buddy's Run to Four Points Lodge and then Rainbow to Sundown. Ca-ching went the point tally.

Then it was over to Tomahawk, Baby Powder and Sunshine, our group still miraculously together, before the devilish organizers sent us on a knee- and teeth-rattling run down ungroomed, still frozen Westside. At least it was worth three points instead of one.

It was around this time that we began bumping into other bibbed teams skiing hither and yonder. Some were monitoring the point map and others had it perfectly choreographed. "You're going down, Nelson!" one yelled in passing.

From there it was back up top, where I began to realize that the whole thing was actually a good way to explore your hometown mountain. Ski Snooze Bar? Where the heck's that? Luckily, our ace in the hole was STARS volunteer Bill Sawer, who moved here in 1968 and helped fell the logs for the original Four Points hut. The wily Mount Werner veteran knew that it was off to skier's left of Morningside, which we hit after air-filled Hot Cakes.

Next, it was time to brave the Chutes, which thankfully had softened a hair. But not so much that YVB employee Nika didn't kick off a ski and watch it plummet all the way to the bottom.

Which brings up my advice for point-earning categories to add in next year. Skiing Chute One with one ski ought to count, as should being a good Samaritan, which we did when retrieving a guest's ski. Drinking a Bacon bloody mary at Hazie's might be another good addition, as would earning points for pee stops, feeding the birds at Morningside and kissing a lift op.

Gifted planners that we were, we saved the worst for last: a slow, slush- and skate-filled run down Why Not from top to bottom (three points), and another even slower more tortuous pole down flat-as-a-pancake BC Skiway (three more). Hey organizers, what are you, sadomasochists?

When all was said and done and we ended our crusade just before the 2 p.m. cutoff at Slopeside Grill, our final score tallied 140. While that was respectable, it paled to the winning 161 points recorded by Paula's Posse, who must have strapped their tracking device to a lift chair for an extra lap or two. And while Yampa Valley Bank's fundraising effort of $4,500 was certainly commendable (despite Wharton's "Never Trust a Banker" T-shirt), it was local Steve Williams' team topping the donation list at $11,000.

But the real winner, besides those owning stock in Bengay and that Tired Old Ass Soak body elixir, was STARS, which raised $90,000 from the event for its year-round programs. If only I could get some similar support for my aching knees.

A Stand-up Act

The back of Andy Campbell's orange, fiberglass-shelled Praschberger mono-ski reads "Die Living." He's doing a good job.

He just flew 20 feet off a jump, bounced 20 more, and is now lying on his side below a wind lip in the backcountry of Buffalo Pass. The impact sheared the bolts off his sit-ski and, like a turtle, he's unable to move.

"That should have held up through that," he says, as guides Humpty Dumpty him back together and eventually toboggan him back to the snowcat waiting below.

Campbell's here for the first-ever Legends of the Deep Powder Exhibition, an event taking some of the world's best adaptive skiers into the backcountry for something hard to find in lift-accessed terrain: untracked powder. Waiting at the snowcat are three other sit-skiers, two three-track skiers (one-legged skiers), and visually impaired skier Luanne Burke, with her guide.

Campbell, 32, is used to the fuss. Three months after returning from the Iraq invasion with the British Army, a climbing accident sent him 65 feet to the ground and to life in a wheelchair. While in the hospital for seven months, he thought of mountain sports he might still be able to pursue; skiing and paragliding quickly schussed to the surface. He became a certified pilot, and eventually landed on the British Disabled Ski Team. He looked like he combined the two sports off that last air.

"Let's stay away from trees and rocks," guide Kent Vertrees said earlier. "The number one goal is to stay safe."

His preface has reason.

"I promise not to push my tibia up into my knee again," answered 14-year sit-skier Lucien Smith, 43, paralyzed from the waist down in a motocross accident at age 19.

He then launched into a story about breaking his toe last summer, but not knowing how.

"U.D.I.," chimed in Craig Kennedy, founder of Access Anything, which organized today's event with Steamboat Powdercats. "Unidentified Drinking Injury."

Smith broke his tibia here two years ago in the backcountry at the end of Access Anything's annual adaptive skiers camp by sit-skiing into a hidden rock. He skied four more runs and didn't realize it was broken until that night in the shower. So he took a Valium, drank a beer, and called a taxi to take him to the hospital.

But Smith wouldn't trade the backcountry for the world, broken bones, toe-teasings and all. "I don't have the tolerance to wait around and run gates," he says. "And that's the only real avenue available to adaptive skiers. The idea of getting us out in the backcountry is awesome."

While today's event is just an exhibition, it marks the first time Access Anything has brought skiers with disabilities into such challenging terrain. Hence, Vertrees's word of caution. They don't want anything to jeopardize plans to turn it into a competition, with participants vying for the title of best adaptive powder skier in the world.

"It's all about skiing with friends and having a good time," says Kennedy, a paraplegic after breaking nine vertebrae in a skiing accident in 1994. "A lot of people don't think we can compete on this level, but we can." In the cat, the guides make their introductions.

"I'm Pete," says Pete Scully, handing out avalanche beacons and tracing our route on a topo map.

"That's Pete, also," answers participant Ron McMorris, pointing to his fake leg. "Pete the Peg."

Shortly later, the cat doors open and everyone files out, the two mono-skiers sitting in the aisle sliding backwards down a wooden ramp. Before them: acres of untracked lines, soon to be riddled with three-track signatures.

If they didn't know it before, they do now: face shots come a lot easier when you're sitting only two feet off the ground. But powder is tougher to ski than it is for the stand-up crowd. "You can't hop or un-weight," says Smith, a skier for 15 years before his accident. "Without knees, it's harder to push it around."

Still, grins are as wide as our cat tracks as we ski lap after lap. On the last run, everyone soars off the wind lip, Campbell paragliding father than even the able-bodied guides. For the guides, it's their best trip of the year. They've never seen clients so happy to be alive.

Later, at the awards party, prizes are given out for Best Line, Air, Crash and Face Shot. Campbell wins the air and crash categories hands down. A prize is also given out for Best Lack of Face Shot, which goes to the peg-legged McMorris, who lost his leg after crashing his motorcycle into an earthmover at age 16. His three-track outriggers make him too tall.

Campbell sinks a combo shot at the pool table and then wheels to the far side to line up another. "Skiing isn't supposed to be about sliding down a race course for a medal," he says, eyeing his next shot. "It's about getting into the mountains and enjoying life, one face shot at a time."

The Storm That Town Forgot

Okay, somebody's gotta' say something, so it might as well be me. For all the marvelous snowpack it provided, the storm just before the resort's opening day in 2015 was a bit of a let down. A three-day dump gets everyone's hopes up for one of the best openings ever, and then "freezing rain" crusts it over to the consistency of burnt crème brulee.

It wouldn't have been so bad if it weren't such a complete surprise. Everyone's collective powder juices were flowing like the Yampa for the resort's opening Scholarship Day, fueled all the more by a bonus, 15-inch dump on Tuesday. But then came the Great Glaze, decimating it in a single downpour.

It was like the Broncos in the 2014 Super Bowl, which they lost 43-8 to the Seahawks; all sorts of built-up expectations, only to flop flat on their faces. Which is exactly what happened to unsuspecting skiers as soon as they got off the lift, traversed over to White Out and attempted their first turn. Their skis sunk below the crust, couldn't get back up, and Wham! went each and every skier face-first into the offending medium. It's as if someone pointed a giant spray gun at Routt County and shellacked the entire snowpack into a gleaming sheen.

On the bright side, it wasn't the worse opening day ever. There was tons of coverage, and the groomers skied pretty well. But it was the wackiest. Where low snow years serve up a lone ribbon of death to ski on, this year the whole mountain was that ribbon. It was everywhere except where they groomed. Skiing off-piste wasn't worth the knee cartilage it consumed.

It left locals shaking their heads as to how so much snow could go to crap so quickly overnight. What did we do to upset Ullr and deserve that? Grass the Nordic jumps?

I skinned the mountain just the day before, as did countless others, and it skied great. Then, whammo!, overnight the entire mountain was crustier than former LA Clippers owner Donald Sterling. Those lucky enough to ski it before Elsa the Snow Queen waved her snow-ruining wand had their tracks frozen in time and enshrined for all to see. The tracks already there from before the Great Freeze were as ghostly as Planet of the Apes, a relic of a former soft snow civilization. Especially since an ensuing warm spell preserved them for all eternity, as if rubbing it in our faces. It's the longest fresh tracks have ever lasted on the mountain. Even now, a week later, no one dares cross them.

It was as bad as anyone's ever seen it, from the Werners to the Withers. "I was lucky to get out alive," said a friend who ignored caution and ducked into closed Closets. "Even traversing out was hairball."

Sure, we've had wind crust before, and even a fluke rain or two. But nothing like this. It had patrollers in conniptions wondering how to deal with pent-up-powder-fever-meets-instant-curveball-by-Mother-Nature.

And the incident could have long-term repercussions as well, breaking loose avalanches as well as legs. That layer, or "rain event" if you want to sound avi-savvy, could well be there all season long, threatening to slide.

Those who didn't fall prey to the Siren's call of untracked knew something was amiss before even setting foot to snow. You could see a weird sheen on the snow everywhere, just daring you to dive in. On the lift, you could hear it creak and groan. It didn't sound like normal powder. Tree clumps landed with an audible clank before shattering into shards. If this didn't raise a red flag, your sense of sight did. Sheets of ice fractured by those braving the Forbidden Zone tobogganed alongside them down the hill. A pair of sunglasses took a luge ride all the way down Tornado, one lens missing from the beating. A set of tracks down the face was nothing more than a series of open quotation marks, penetrating through every five feet before ending in a massive crater.

It didn't take a PhD. to heed the lift shack advice to stick to groomed terrain—even the man-made snow seemed soft, a home base where you could re-circle the wagons. My kids and I braved one turn into the quarantined zone only to Brave Sir Robin it back out as quickly as we entered. The crusty layer was the Great Equalizer, bringing every skier or rider down to the same ass-over-teakettle level. Shame of all shames, it even blocked the direct route to the Slopeside bar to commiserate afterward.

And it wasn't just on the mountain. It was all over, like some sort of plague. From town, the Valley View run glistened menacingly in the sun. North toward Buff Pass and south toward the Flat Tops, the goading gleam was the same. And it affected backcountry recreation of all walks. No one dared venture off Blackmere Drive when climbing Emerald or thought about touring Walton Peak since it arrived. It's all contaminated like the red tide. We got Grinched, plain and simple, every last Who down in Skiville.

Still, we shouldn't complain since most of the time we get our trademark

Champagne Circle-R powder. And, spoiled as we are, it makes us appreciate how good we have it here in Ski Town USA. Besides, the resort is slowly beating it back, inch by groomed inch, packing out the offending film like controlling a fire. And the groomers are skiing great for so early in the season.

We just have to turn the other cheek (giving Mother Nature a collective moon in the process) and put our best foot forward, hopefully not breaking through the stratum in the process.

Epilogue

What a difference a storm can make. One day we're languishing in the remnants of the worst snow layer ever and the next, voila!, a 20-inch storm wallops Mount Werner into submission, popping the celebratory cork on full-blown, Steamboat-style Champagne.

After two weeks of being painstakingly beaten down by the sun and the wildfire-like combat efforts of side-stepping ski instructors, the evil sheen that had so disgruntled everyone was knocked out by a storm from the same heavens that wracked us with the "freezing rain." It was as if Mother Nature herself reached down and said, "You have suffered enough, my minions, now rejoice and enjoy my bounty."

It was the only elixir that could've salvaged the season. It's as if someone took a giant can of Crust Begone and pointed it at Mount Werner, blanketing the offending film with fluff. It was Good vs. Evil, with the victory needle swaying toward benevolence.

Lift ops smiled, PR wonks Instagrammed and skiers and riders high-fived. In one fell swoop, the storm placated town's pent-up powder jones. The windfall also caused closet crustologists to sound off on a new round of pontifications. Those who claimed it would be here all year were forced to recant. Those espousing on temperature gradients, crystal bonding and isothermic layering put their thermometers back in their pocket protectors. All theories were swept aside thanks to one storm.

Of course, people still skied it tentatively, dipping their toes in the water before plunging in. Was that hideous crust layer really gone? For good? It was like one of those horror films featuring a creature lurking below the surface, like "Piranha," "Anaconda," or even "Snow Shark" (yes, there is such a thing). But it was hasta la vista for the denizen of the deep, thanks to the ski area's SWAT-like packing regime and 20 saving-grace inches of fluff.

Of course, it's still down there somewhere, a tree ring reminding us of the subpar start to the season. Avi-archaeologists digging pits will find it, and backcountry travelers will have to tread lightly all season long. But for the on-piste persuasion, the season's savior was born in a storm that kicked ol' Crust Kringle in the derriere, heralding a collective Hallelujah just in time for the holidays. And there was much rejoicing.

The 12 Days of Christmas, Steamboat-style

Forget the partridge in a pear tree, turtle doves and drummers drumming. How about we all get the 12 days of Christmas, Steamboat-style? To wit (try to read without singing), on the first day of Christmas my true love gave to me...

1. Scratch the Partridge in a Pear Tree. How about we go with Powder in the Bear Trees. This is named for a secret spot us backcountry aficionados go to on Buff Pass for unequivocal powder turns. And there's no bird poop to scoop up.

2. Instead of Two Turtle Doves, how about something more practical, like Two Marmot Gloves, from that new Marmot store downtown operated by the resort—perfect for those frigid, hand-circling, subzero winter weekends. In particular, how about the Randonee, made from Thermal R synthetic, with soft fingers for those chairlift nose wipes.

3. Sorry, French Hens, you're outta here. Let's go with three cups of that spoon-slurping French Onion soup from Carl's Tavern. You know, the one with three different types of onions, port wine reduction, a Mount Werner-sized crouton and gruyere cheese.

4. Calling Birds? Really? How about calls from the powder report hotline (970-879-7300), automatically programmed to dial you whenever it dumps eight inches or more? We can even let it have that little calling bird whistle as the ringtone.

5. Say it loud and say it proud (with the proper hesitation): Five Golden Leafs! Gift certificates, that is, for everything under the indica and sativa sun. And you wonder why Santa is always so jolly and laughing all the time, and eating those platefuls of cookies.

6. Geese-a-Laying? Sounds like a lot of honking and turd-cleaning. Just ask our neighbors, Shelli and Shawn. Instead of a goose-a-laying, let's go with For Moose-We're-Praying , sending our best wishes for a speedy recovery to town icon Moose Barrows.

7. Swans-a-Swimming conjures up a pretty sight, but where will they go come winter? Old Town Hot Springs? (You ever notice that these gifts include a lot of birds?) For this one, let's try Sans-Clothes-Swimming at the Strawberry Park Hot Springs. After dark, of course, to hide my swan-white belly.

8. Maids-a-Milking. How about we settle for Maple Bacon Donuts at Milk Run/Moose Watch Café? Those things are seriously the bomb, blood pressure be damned. Though eat too many and you won't have to worry about too many maids coming around.

9. Ladies Dancing. Not much to dislike here, especially for all the male ski bums in town. But how about we get a few more shaking their stuff at Schmiggity's? And perhaps some more Ladies Nights and Two-step Tuesdays?

10. Let's replace Lords-a-Leaping (which sounds slightly feminine and flappy-panted) with Skiers-a-Jumping on the newly restored 90-meter jump at Howelsen Hill (thanks Gerber-Berend Design Build). Bonus present: the new terrain park at the former tubing hill.

11. Pipers Piping. This one begs a call-out to construction workers finally finishing the storm pipes on Yampa Street. So let's give them some extra elf-power to actually finish before Santa takes to the skies next holiday season.

12. Drummers Drumming aren't bad, as long as you're not hungover. But since we have the world's only marching band on skis right here every Winter Carnival, let's give them some a-rumpa-pum-pum love with some Steamboat earmuffs for those frigid temps, and some Vaseline for those poor, lip-on-metal tuba players. And, oh yeah, some more African drum nights at the Steamboat Arts Depot.

Working Lift Lines

With the "Gondola Line Starts Here" sign starting around One Steamboat Place, a few hundred yards from where you get on, I could tell Monday was going to be a doozy—one that would call upon every lift line negotiating skill I had ever honed.

Fortunately, it's an art form we don't have to practice often in Steamboat. Skiers in Vail are much better versed at it than we are, as are the Euros, who have no problem stubbing their cigarettes out on your helmet as they shuffle over your skis in one-piece suits. But when we do get lines here—say, hypothetically, when a record 27 inches falls the night before Presidents' Day—you want to place your best boot forward, cutting for holes like a running back and assessing options like a stockbroker, all while maintaining a modicum of mountain-town politeness.

Luckily, there are ways to milk the system. So while it may jeopardize my own line juggling, behold a few tricks of the work-the-maze trade.

Rule No. 1: Head to where the lines aren't. At the supermarket, you don't head to the cashier with three carts; you pick the short line. Do the same on the slopes; avoid lines from the get-go. Skin up early, sign up for First Tracks or persuade your loved one to drop you off at the bottom of Thunderhead Express. But since I had as fat a chance of that happening as eating a crawfish correctly on the coming Fat Tuesday, I was left to my own line-dodging devices.

As part of this tenet, scout out your options before committing to one queue and always have a Plan B. Line at Storm Peak Express? Head to 4 Points or Pony Express. (Hint: Scout the Storm line at 4 Points and Pony at Storm). Just know that if you get burned at Pony, you're left with a long slog back to Thunderhead.

Rule No. 2: Embrace the singles line, even if there's more than one skier in your party. I did this with my kids a few days earlier, ushering them into the singles line at the gondola. My youngest, Casey, protested possibly riding alone, but in the end, it all worked out as we were ushered into the same car. This, too, requires assessment and quick math; sometimes the multi-person line might prove faster.

Rule No. 3: All else being equal, pick the line closest to the loading zone; it's more direct. That way you're that many rows ahead when it comes time to load. By the end of the day (assuming your legs last that long), this could add up to an entire run.

Rule No. 4: Look for friends ahead of you. That surfaced when I heard a friend call out my name up ahead. So we scootched forward, semi-Euro-style, but with a legitimate alibi ("Uh, excuse us, we're with them," we feebly proffered). We leapfrogged forward a whole two spots this way, which, given the alternations, added up significantly.

Rule No. 5: Always look to better your position (especially on quads and six-packs). To do this, pair up with another couple ahead of you, not behind. And encourage others to make pairs ahead of you, under the guise of good Samaritanship. And feel free to leapfrog. After joining my friend's crew for 10 minutes, we saw a lone foursome farther ahead and jumped ship to slingshot forward. "Thanks for the bump," I said, as we bid my friend adieu.

Rule No. 6: All lines being equal, choose one that lets you ski a run. Figuring the lines at Sundown Express and Storm Peak would be the same, we skied White Out to Storm, instead of a catwalk to Sundown. The face shots soon faced us with another choice: 4 Points or Storm? Back to Rule No. 1. Since the Storm line looked manageable and earned us more vert, we headed to its far side. There, we got lucky again, sliding in with a couple ahead of us.

Rule No 7: While waiting for others, wait in line. Then you're killing two birds. Let your partners slide forward to catch you.

Rule No. 8: Check the alternating pattern. Some lines alternate more times than others; if they're the same length, that puts you exponentially back. Hint: Outside lines are often faster than inside ones because they merge less. Plus, they let your partners easily join you once they arrive.

Rule No. 9: Have a mark or control group to test your line theory. Ours was that tall guy in the neon green jacket and red helmet one line over. He was ahead of us at the get-go, but we passed him with his own flying colors. We lapped that far line four times before a maze technician finally threw in a few more merges.

Rule No. 10: When it comes to waiting, there are no friends on powder days.

W · A · T · E · R

A Canine Canoe Rescue

I was reading Sky, the Blue Fairy to my 4-year-old daughter when the call came. "It's Johnny," my wife, Denise, said. "Something about a dog."

I hesitated. Any call from Johnny could only lead to trouble. He was always getting me into trouble.

"Want to do another dorky line?" he asked as I picked up the phone, referring to the small ski shots we leave our tracks on around town.

I peered out the window. It was a Tuesday night in mid-September at 10 p.m., pitch black, with the porch thermometer barely nudging 40 degrees. It was also a school night, for crying out loud. But Johnny kept talking. "How about a nighttime paddle with cops lighting the river for us?"

Heavy rains had brought the Elk River to almost triple its normal flow, and two dogs, he said, a chocolate and yellow lab, had somehow fallen off a cliff onto a narrow ledge. They were trapped between the cliff and the rising water, and one of the dogs was badly hurt. The other one wouldn't leave his buddy's side.

Johnny, who lives nearby, was already on the scene, as were a gaggle of first responders puzzling out a plan to lower a fire-truck ladder to the dogs. But Johnny had a better idea. All he needed was a willing accomplice—one who owned a canoe.

I hung up, put Sky the Blue Fairy back on the bedstand, kissed my daughter good night and strapped my 16-foot Old Town canoe onto the truck.

The bridge a few hundred yards downstream of the trapped dogs was a mass of flashing emergency lights when I arrived. A solitary beam—normally reserved for perps, not pets—caught the glow from two sets of frightened eyes, stranded between the high limestone cliff and a ribbon of whitewater.

Blocking my expired tags with my knee, I introduced myself to the two sheriff's deputies on site, who helped us unload the canoe and pass it over the guardrail. They then gave us their Kevlar gloves and black, police-issue flashlights to help with the cause. Once on the other side of the fence, Johnny and I carried the boat upstream to a spot where we could ferry across the swollen river to the courageous canines trapped on the far bank.

With police floodlights from the bridge both blinding us and showing us the way, we paddled hard for the far bank, carefully entering the eddy next to the ledge harboring the dogs. The injured yellow lab looked up despondently as we arrived. His friend wriggled with happiness.

That's when it hit me. The faithful chocolate represented what we value most in a backcountry partner, be it hunting, backpacking, skiing or paddling: loyalty. He had scrambled around the cliff to see if his partner was OK, barked to get people's attention, and never left his friend's side.

As we pulled the canoe onto the ledge, I remembered a similar situation I had once been in while kayaking Clear Creek on the Front Range. I'd missed a move and was pinned against a midstream rock. Unable to free myself, my fate was entirely in my friend Eric's hands. He leapt out of his boat, scrambled upstream and plunged into the river to free me. Neither of us thought much of it at the time—helping a buddy in need is at the core of all outdoor sports—but the chocolate's loyalty was a welcome reminder.

"That's right…You're a good little adventure buddy," I said, patting his Cro-Magnon head before wrapping a blanket around his injured partner and hoisting him into the canoe. Then we eased the canoe into the dark, fast-moving water, leaving Loyal Boy to swim behind.

The police lights blinded us again as we picked our way downstream through backlit waves. As if at an interrogation table, I felt the need to make a confession. Have I been as loyal a backcountry partner as the chocolate was to his Old Yeller? Have I been appreciative enough to those who have helped me? As we passed under the police and slid safely into an eddy below the bridge, I vowed to do better on both counts.

The deputies whisked both dogs to the vet in a squad car, and as they drove away I could see the trusty chocolate pressing his nose through the rear grate toward his friend. In the morning I learned that the yellow's name was Donyek, and that he now had casts on both front feet, en route to a full recovery. His faithful buddy's name was Kobe.

The next day the newspaper ran a story on the rescue titled "Doggone Kindness." While I wasn't really interested in the accolades—I'm always up for an adventure with Johnny and will take any excuse to avoid Sky, the Blue Fairy—this midnight mission offered more than that. It renewed my appreciation of what it means to be a good wingman or woman.

The next morning I called Eric and thanked him for staying by my side on Clear Creek all those years before. "No problem," he replied. "That's what partners are for."

Circumnavigating Howelsen Hill

"Cool tent," said my friend Bill Gamber. "Who makes it?"

His interest in the rolled-up UPS parcel was natural; he runs a tent company called Big Agnes, and the 4-pound package was lighter than many of his offerings.

"It's not a tent," I answered, unfurling the stuff sack's contents over the floor. "It's a new type of raft."

Spilled onto the carpet, the raft's deflated, crinkly material didn't look suitable for the hot springs pool, let alone the wilderness. But I knew differently. Made by Alaskan grandmother Sheri Tingey, Alpacka rafts weigh less than the six-packs tubers carry down the Yampa—a whopping 30 pounds less than the next lightest inflatable kayak on the market—and are opening up the backcountry to unprecedented exploration. The company sells nearly 1,000 a year to paddlers, trekkers, hunters, fishermen and hikers. Adventure racers camp under them, and bush pilots stash them under their seats for emergencies.

Bill raised his eyebrows, not overly impressed. "What's that?" he asked, pointing to a funnel-shaped piece of nylon. "It looks like a hat."

The "hat" was its 2-ounce pump, another ingeniously lightweight invention. Screwing the spout's threads onto the valve, I lifted the funnel's sides, filled it with air, and bellowed the craft to life. In five minutes, the raft's form filled the office with an oval inner tube, complete with an attached spray skirt.

"It's revolutionizing the sport," I said proudly. "People are taking these things everywhere."

Proof, I knew, lay in the exploits of adventurers like Alaska's Roman Dial, who just published a 790-trip guidebook for them. He's used them for such off-the-wall expeditions as an 800-mile traverse of the Alaska Range, and a monthlong, four-river, tundra-crossing through the Brooks Range to the Beaufort Sea. Five climbers once even packrafted into the Yukon Territory's famed Cirque of the Unclimbables, carrying everything they needed—from provisions to climbing gear—for their 20-day, dual-sport adventure.

With a permanently attached spray skirt, hardcores are also using them in whitewater. Hardshell converts Sam Perry and Nathan Shoutis once bounced them down Washington's 820-foot-per-mile Dingford Creek, which makes Mad Creek look like Fetcher Pond. Tourers are catching the craze as well, with Erin McKittrick and Brent Higman using them, believe it or not, on a 4,000-mile hiking/packrafting/skiing journey from Seattle to the Aleutian Islands.

But paddling is believing. So with the Yampa River still lined with ice, I set out to test it locally for a review for Men's Journal magazine. To do so, I needed to hike with it, rig it in the field and paddle it. Problem was, the mountains were still covered in snow and the river mostly frozen. That's when the light bulb struck: I'd take it on a first-ever skate-ski/raft circumnavigation of Howelsen Hill right out my backdoor—just the sort of wacky trip they were designed for.

Filing my itinerary with the appropriate authorities (i.e. my wife), I loaded my drysuit, raft, PFD and breakdown paddle in a drybag—even throwing in a sleeping bag for better wilderness simulation. Then I skate-skied southeast from my home in Fairview up Blackmere Drive and onto the Howelsen Nordic trails.

Never mind the odd looks that got flashed my way by the lycra-clad Bjorns and Svens passing me on their skate skis as I languished uphill, paddle blades sticking out of my backpack and rising over my head like antlers. I kept my head down—both in embarrassment and to help my cardio—and plodded on.

Eventually I made it up and over and onto the final groomed switchback on the Bluffs Loop. There I bravely ventured off-piste and traversed down to River Road and finally the river.

If possible, I felt even dorkier than I did getting passed by skate skiers as I skied up to a pair of fly fishermen and pulled the raft out of my pack. As they looked on incredulously, I then inflated it with the bellows, struggled into my drysuit, fastened my skis atop the craft with a bungee and climbed inside.

I was now wearing a bathtub—at six feet, its measurements aren't far off—with only my daughter's rubber ducky missing. Like most newbie packrafters, I couldn't help but giggle as I set off paddling what surely belongs in a cartoon.

This, of course, all fits into their design. "You can't get too serious in them," maintains Tingey. "There's something almost childlike about them, like a glorified inner tube you can actually control. They make you feel like a kid again."

Tingey, a ski suit seamstress originally from Jackson, Wyoming, invented the craft in 2000 when her son, Thor, asked her to build a boat for a trip in the Brooks Range. She built 30 by 2002 before outsourcing production to Jack's Plastic Welding, and later to Vancouver's Feathercraft. I was now putting the fifth-generation through its packraft paces.

Testing the durability of its urethane-coated nylon, I bounced off a snowbank near Backdoor Sports as if it was aufeis in the Arctic. The fact that the craft has only one air chamber—its only real pitfall—surfaced briefly, but it paid the abrasion no mind. Next, I tested the claim that it draws only three inches of water by scraping over some cobblestones in the Double Z shallows. Again, the craft passed by like the Roadrunner outsmarting Wile E. Coyote.

Then came the clencher: punching Charlie's Hole by the library. Though more weight up front—picture Fred Flintstone's brontosaurus rack at the drive-in—would offer better counter-balance, I made it through fine to the gawks of fishermen and passersby.

Circumnavigation completed after the D-hole, I rolled up the raft in front of an elderly couple parked by the Depot in a brown Buick Century with Wyoming plates. Without even trying to explain what I had done, I shouldered my skis and hiked the two blocks home.

In all, I had traveled a circle of five miles door to door—a far cry from Dial's exploits but it proved that the rafts have a place, even in Routt County (especially after I began hiking them in to fish high alpine lakes). It also proved their worth to Bill, who happened to drive by while I was hiking home with skis, drybag, raft, and paddle. "Way to go, Eug," he shouted from his window. "Looks like people really are taking those things everywhere."

Injurious Kayak

The kayak hasn't progressed much since I last saw it. Resting atop two sawhorses in my neighbor's backyard, it looks the same as it did when he put it away for the winter last fall—a lacey, pine frame still awaiting is final skin.

That it has resurfaced after its winter hibernation is testament to the fact that spring is in the air. The ritual of moving it from his basement to backyard is as much a harbinger of the changing seasons as the ducks flying north overhead.

This year I have a much better view of it than in years past. Knee surgery from playing Jonny Moseley in the Howelsen halfpipe with kids half my age has confined me to our living room's corner couch, from which I can see every nuance of the neighborhood. Without much else to do besides watch Woods win the Players Championships, Agassi defeat Rafter in the Ericsson Open, and Arizona topple Illinois in the NCAA round of eight, I can study the surroundings in detail. The snow bank between our homes has melted to expose a long-lost yard (and long-lost canine landmines). The creek has started gurgling again, coursing through budding cottonwoods on its way to the river. The birds have started chirping, reminders of which lie plastered on the driveway.

The kayak is a thing of beauty. After a week of watching my neighbor hunch over it, I hobble over to pay him a visit, my lone crutch sinking into the spring-saturated soil. It's the third season he's worked on it, patterning it after plans he saw in a book called Wood and Canvas Kayak Building. He stripped the wood for it himself from two-by-sixes pilfered from a construction site, and then built it in his basement. He had to shove it through his basement window to get it out in the yard. At night, when he isn't working on it, he covers it with a green tarp and coils an orange extension cord around its bow.

When I arrive, he's putting on a layer of shellac and debating what type of material to use as a skin. Anxious to test its Greenland-style hull, he covered it last fall with a temporary layer of 8mm visqueen and took it for a test spin on a local lake. Overloaded with two people in an open-style cockpit, the boat handled poorly, nearly capsizing when wind chop scoured the surface. He spent the week I watched from my window adding cross ribs and shrinking the cockpit so he wouldn't be tempted to try such folly again.

He offers me a beer and we talk about hull shapes, tracking, skin materials, rudders and paddles. He walks me through the kayak's lines, running his hand over the intricate frame. He is not a "paddler" by any sense of the word; rather, a handyman whose current project will give him an excuse to go out on the water. I tell him I might be able to hook him up with a few accessories to get it seaworthy. "All I need is a beer holder," he says.

By sundown, some of his friends show up and a keg is tapped by a campfire. Soon they'll start their rubber ducky races down the creek: three bucks a duck, with $2 going to the winner and $1 to the keg fund. I return to my corner couch and watch the festivities from afar, a nerdy silhouette outlined in a window. Surrounded by merry-makers fresh out of work for the offseason, the kayak remains a focal point throughout the party. My leg elevated and packed in ice, I flip on the TV to an ad showing a sea kayaker in front of a glacier-capped peak. Keep with it, I think to my neighbor. That will be you soon enough.

Life in a River Town

It's easy to overlook, that ribbon of water coursing through downtown. But that's our local waterway, the Yampa River, and it seeps into our life just as it does the surrounding soil. Nurturing farmland, aquatic habitat, municipalities recreation and more, its pulse becomes your own as it changes from raging torrent to trout-filled trickle. And the longer you live by it the more it becomes a part of who you are.

Chore Conduit

Lunch breaks in a river town can be a little different than they are elsewhere. Consider the time I used the waterway for a personal errand bonanza. It happened after our noon-whistle pierced the air, causing us worker-bees to Flintstone out of our offices. While on a quick nooner kayak run, I realized it was the last day to sign up for summer hockey. So I pulled over, climbed through a willow thicket and walked dripping wet to the registration desk, water spilling off my helmet onto the form.

Back in my boat, it was on to Pete's riverside outdoor shop, where I yelled through the backdoor. Discussing details for an upcoming family camping trip, we decided I'd shop breakfasts and he'd take dinners. Back on the water, I saw my plumber walking by. Our basement had flooded and I asked him how the trouble-shooting was coming; he'd be over to help me snake my drain tiles the next day. Next stop was Bamboo Market, where I dripped over to buy fruit and vegetables for home, stashing them beneath my spray skirt. Four chores and a kayak run, all in an hour-and-a-half —a tad long should a Brontosaurus from the Flintstones punch my time card, but not bad for lunch break.

Royal Coachman to Coaching

In late June, just before the river breathes its last gasp, a two-week window arrives for prime float fishing. That's when the dories come out, anglers casting streamers, dries and hopper-droppers into the receding waters.

The call came from Johnny St. John, who owns driftboat company Hog Island Boatworks. By 3:30 p.m., I was bailing on work and winching his dory into the river. We took turns casting and rowing, leaving no eddy line untouched. I landed three browns before realizing time had gotten away. It was 4:50 and I needed to coach my daughter's soccer team at 5.

So I abandoned ship mid-float. Still clad in my fishing vest, I waded through the willows up onto River Road and stuck out my thumb, getting a ride from the first driver—a thirty-something gal who didn't mind my wet sandals or bulging vest. And that's how she dropped me off, after I convinced her to take me straight to the field. I arrived five minutes late, still likely the only coach to show up with wooly-buggers hanging next to his whistle.

Tubing Time

It happens every year. Kayakers and rafters get the river all spring, but then comes the Great Transition. As the rocks re-appear, so does the rubber; the hatch is on and river gets turned over to…tubers.

For a short time the two camps overlap. The water is waning, but there's still enough for kayakers and stand-up paddleboarders to surf, playing Space Invaders by dodging tubers as they bumble downstream.

You can't help but harbor a degree of animosity toward them. They're not your kind. They have mullets and gold chains. They drag coolers. They have no control. They wear bikinis and board shorts instead of being armored in spray skirt, PFD and helmet.

But then you find yourself one of them, part of arm-circling Americana with daughter in lap and triceps chafed from arm flutters. And it occurs to you that it's easy and fun, especially if you come to it with a paddling background. You can ferry away from obstacles and avoid butt-bruising shallows.

You feel somehow superior to them—the boy in the vinyl inflatable kayak from Whamco, the couple dangling fingers from an inflatable mattress, the two cotton-clad girls paddling an inflatable swimming pool. What really separates you is The Hole, where you're now the semi in Frogger, mowing down kayakers trying to cross the freeway. You punch through, hoping none of your boater buddies recognizes you. That's when you see Blakesly, a kayaker back in town from college, snorkeling for tuber bootie. "Four pairs of sunglasses, a Nets visor and half bottle of cinnamon schnapps," he brags, holding up his trophies.

Then you walk with your daughter back up the bike path. "My dad's a tuber," she proudly states to the first passerby. Despite their mullets and Michelins, it's all enjoying yourself on the river.

The Fever

The indicators appear everywhere—a melting-snow puddle in the alley, water trickling down curbs and disappearing into grates, icicles metronoming out the office window, lawn clutter and dog landmines re-emerging from snow-covered yards. On the river, an ice dam vanishes that was there the day before. A spring smell comes to the air, thick with moisture.

Ads for boating gear appear in the classifieds. Chairlift conversations turn to percent-of-average snowpack. You stop ignoring the pull-up bar in the garage and watch your mailbox for permit responses. Boaters you haven't seen since fall start crawling out of the winter woodwork, rubbing their eyes to greet spring. You see them at coffee shops, parking lots and taverns, talk turning to what's flowing where. They're all afflicted with the same malady: Boating Fever.

Conveniently, it comes at a lull in other recreational pursuits, before trails dry for biking and after the ski season has melted away. Soon you're looking for your equipment again, realizing you never repaired that neck gasket or fixed that wetsuit bootie zipper.

Then you try to remember how to run shuttle. Let's see…if we leave Auto A here and Bike B there, then we can all pile in Car C and go to Point D…but then we won't have Car C once we get to Point E, so let's leave it here.

Eventually you feel the first splash of the season. You're paddling again. And then the frenzy ensues. Everything else gets shoved to the back burner… family, jobs, house projects, legs, wives, even your wife's legs. Cardio-vascular turns to mush and winter-honed quadriceps reduce to toothpicks, but you don't care. You'll suffer at the end of the bike pack later on. Dinner isn't served until 9 p.m. Spouses grumble. They don't understand. The water's finite, coursing downstream without you.

Soon the dreaded brown patch appears on the mountain. Then it connects with another, signaling the river's peak. You get in your last licks. And then, like that, it's over; the water fades away, just like your clique of friends that paddle it—but it'll be back next year.

An Affair with Floods

It's an odd scene. My Dutch oven, which I'd last used it to bake a pineapple upside-down cake, is mocking the Archimedes Principle (for an object to float, its weight must be less than that of the water it displaces). It's floating in a foot of water in my basement crawlspace, and giving a passenger a ride. Inside is a half-full bottle of Crisco, getting ferried like the giggling Pillsbury Doughboy from the flooded bikes in the corner toward a saturated stroller on the far wall.

I feel like I'm in Night at the Museum. Everything has come to life—five-gallon water jugs, ground pads and even my three kayaks —all floating and bumping into each other, as if released from Sleeping Beauty's slumber. It's a homeowner's nightmare. Our basement—repository of a lifetime collection of outdoor gear—hasn't flooded ever. Now it's turned Dutch ovens into passenger ferries. Any ordinary person would be calculating the property loss. But another thought flashes through my mind: It's going to be a helluva big water year. The snowpack is at 260 percent of last year's, with Mount Werner bursting with an unheard-of 130-inch base.

If Mr. Floating Doughboy portends the paddling season, so does my rafting gear outside. We're leaving on a trip in two days, but my frame and oars are entombed in ice along the side of house. It will take three hours of pick-axing, profanities and vats of boiling water to free them.

Our trip mate, Leeann, has it worse. She stowed her gear in her hatch-accessed basement all winter. To free it, she had to host an impromptu, snow-melting, gear-freeing bonfire party, placing the fire over the trap door.

Most people in town are worried. There's a run on sandbags at ACE Hardware, and stories in the paper on how to avoid water damage. But they're seeing the Yin instead of the Yang.

Wading into the snowmelt, I grab a kayak as it floats past and nudges my Dutch oven into the far corner. I'll sump-pump the mess later; right now I'm going boating.

Truck for Sale

The ad read: "Kayak for Sale. Comes with free shuttle rig. Both a little rusty, but great for around town."

It was my trusty '82 Datsun King Cab 4X4 with shell, stereo and rack. But with 187,000 hard-earned miles, it was time for it to go. The boat was my Perception Dancer, which had served me well back when boats lasted a half decade or more.

It was natural to get rid of them both at the same time. They were from the same era, in equal states of disrepair near the tool shed. Their ailments were strikingly similar. Both had holes on the bottom, the kayak's fixed with a plastic weld, the truck's covered with floorboard wood. Both had duct-taped bows, the kayak's covering a piton scar, the truck's supporting the grill. And both had dented shells. My insurance company had totaled the truck not once, but twice.

When my wife said the larger of the two eyesores had to go, I popped in a new battery and fired it up. It strained and came to life as if gasping for air, but like a stubborn llama refused to move. Walking around to the tailgate, I saw the reason. As if it, too, realized its fate was imminent, my kayak had wedged itself between shed and tire. Perhaps it had seen me carry new boats into the garage, outfitting them with tender loving care—just as the truck had seen our affections turn to our garage-heated Subaru. Like Rudolph's misfit toys, they were alone and unwanted.

The phone didn't exactly ring off the hook. One person was frightened away by the rust. A 16-year-old showed up with allowance money. But then a rancher named Curt called, looking for something to handle rough terrain. He offered me $200 and then asked about the kayak. He'd never been in one and had a pond on the ranch. Reluctantly, I loaded it onto the rack and never saw either again.

Taking a Stand

When you live in a river town, sometimes you have to stand up for it. I did by driving to Denver to argue against Senate Bill 62, which called for a 350 cubic-feet-per-second cap on recreational water releases.

Earlier, the city had filed for and won a Recreational In-Channel Diversion (RICD) water right, establishing recreation as a beneficial use of the river's water. Now we were fighting for how many drops that meant.

I wasn't supposed to take the stand right off the bat. Like setting a baseball line-up, our plan was to have our heavy-hitters testify first. But they called me to open, so I was the lead-off man testifying in front of Colorado's House Committee on Agriculture. Making matters worse: I had to do so after such big-league proponents as water attorneys and agriculture commissioners.

We were all a little bleary, having sat through five hours of other bill hearings, including one touting the health benefits of raw milk. When Got Milk ended, we took the stand to Get Water. I had a good spiel, reasons why the bill would be detrimental to communities building river parks. Restricting flows to a "one size fits all" cap would be like telling ski areas they have to rely on snow-making instead of Mother Nature. It went well, I thought, until the grilling began.

"Thank you, Mr. Buchanan," the cross-examiner intoned. "With all due respect…are you saying that river running is more important than drinking water?"

I was a deer in the headlights. First at bat and I was thrown a curve ball. "Uh, no," I answered. "In fact, I could use a sip of water right now."

Knowing that RICDs are secondary to existing rights and non-consumptive, meaning the water stays in the river, I survived long enough for our water attorney to take the stand. Two days later the bill was defeated on the House floor. And it saved communities likes ours from being forced to bunt when the basins are loaded.

Death on the River

Live in a river town long enough and it'll happen. You'll lose someone to the river.

It hit closest to home for me a decade ago when friend Chris Delaney died kayaking Gore Canyon. He was a popular fixture in the Steamboat padding scene—organizing trips, pumping his fist whenever you got worked, and trading in his Jeep for a larger shuttle van. He always made a campfire's Final Four.

He had done the run countless times. But this time he flipped in Gore Rapid, hit his head and never wet-exited. The coroner said he died instantly, even though friends chased him far downstream before administering CPR. When I got the call the next morning, my stomach knotted.

The town bonded at his memorial service, evoking the true essence of living in a river town. Friends spoke of his energy, enthusiasm and love of paddling. A table showed collages of him surfing and paddling a raft made of beer kegs. "If you're going to cry," said friend Drew, "do so over the river—maybe it'll rise enough so we can paddle in his honor tomorrow." Emotions ran deeper than the river.

I remember high-fiving him the last time I saw him, just four days earlier teaming-up to play ping pong at a party. We talked about getting together to boat—most likely Gore. And that's what makes his death strike home: It could have been any of us.

It's easy for a non-boater to say he shouldn't have been there. But he should have been, and was—had been a hundred times. A few weeks later I ran the same rapid. Several other paddlers flipped and rolled at the same spot. The move that killed Chris let them pass unscathed. Answers are hard to find.

At the service—held in a park named after Olympian Rich Weiss, another local paddler who died kayaking—we threw flowers into the water and watched them drift like Chris's soul to another land downstream. Later, we threw his ashes into Fish Creek, one of his favorite runs, and watched them get absorbed by the river.

Not Advised: Supping Northgate

Note to self (and others): Don't stand-up paddleboard the North Platte River's Northgate Canyon at 2,600 cubic feet per second. That was the hard-earned take-home from this past weekend, as I finally notched the section off my to-run list, albeit looking more like Mark Spitz than Kelly Slater.

As a kayaker who has lived nearby for two decades, I'd always known the canyon is there, just an hour and a half drive from Steamboat off Colo. Hwy. 125 north of Walden toward Saratoga. But I'd also heard that it's largely flatwater, with just a couple of Class II-III rapids. How wrong I was.

We decided to join friends Kurt and Eva and their two children, Pablo and Luna, all experienced river runners who would be tackling it in a two-person Shredder raft and two kayaks. I, meanwhile, had lined up two stand-up paddleboard buddies, Paul and Adam, to join me. How hard could it be? They were experienced surfers, and I an experienced river runner.

The first harbinger of doom came at the put-in.

"You're not planning to run this in those, are you?" asked a veteran, grizzled, muscle-bound river runner named Monte, who was busy pumping up his custom Maravia cataraft with custom frame and flip lines. "There are a lot of big holes at this level. You guys ever been down this run before?"

No, we hadn't. And indeed, warm temps had brought it up about 1,000 cfs higher than we were expecting, and 1,500 cfs higher than it normally runs this time of year. And Monte was no blow-hard. He's run the Grand Canyon, the Selway, Middle Fork of the Salmon and other whitewater classics. You could hear our collective gulp as far away as his hometown of Rock Springs, Wyoming.

Other people rigging were no more encouraging. Pete and Matt were experienced river runners who had just moved to Laramie from

Durango. While they had never run it, their two teammates had. Both were paddling two-man, self-bailing rafts. "You going in those?" they echoed. We'd come this far, so I guess we were.

Nerves rattling like the rattlesnakes in the nearby sagebrush, we shoved off, getting as much beta as we could beforehand from Monte. The action picks up, he said, after Elk Creek comes in from the right, and the take-out's tricky—make sure to stay way left around an island after the last rapid or you have another 12-mile float.

The river drops about 20 feet per mile, the gradient producing such rapids as Windy Hole, Cowpie, Narrow Falls, Tootsie Roll and Stovepipe. We got an idea of what lay in store at Windy Hole about a mile down, which, at this level, gave a hint of the beefiness lying below.

"That thing had some meat to it," said Kurt once we got through, those of us on SUPs having no qualms dropping to our bellies the entire run simply to survive. "I wonder what that means the downstream ones will be like?"

We'd find out soon enough. Shortly later we saw a raft pulled over at Elk Creek, marking the start of the real action. With Kurt's son Pablo opting out of kayaking, we asked the rafters if they'd mind taking him. The universal river runner help-thy-neighbor credo kicked in and they agreed. All of which opened the door for me to weenie out of supping the rest of the run as well. Rather than have Kurt have to tie Pablo's cumbersome kayak to his tiny two-man raft, I said I could paddle it. That way they'd only have to carry my rolled up inflatable paddleboard instead.

So that's how we ran the rest of the rapids, including the crux of Narrow Falls, which at this level was solid Class IV: me in the relative safety of a kayak and my two unsuspecting cohorts, who had fallen prey to my underselling of the trip, supping it alone. Suffice it to say that by the end of the trip, our newfound friends had one more person and rolled-up paddleboard on their raft, as Paul bailed after his board's fins got ripped off in a nasty swim at Narrow Falls.

And that's how I also found myself buying the beers on the way home for my drowned-rat buddies; sending our third-party-raft-savior Pete a care package of swag as a thank-you gift; and writing notes to self about not supping high water runs.

Ode to the Yampa

The cowboy was clearly in a bind. Wearing the full Louis L'Amour—well-worn jeans, dusty chaps and red bandana—he needed to get himself and horse across the river. We stumbled upon him after rounding a corner during a high-water river trip down Colorado's Yampa Canyon; the only neighborly thing to do was pull over and lend a hand.

His cattle, it seemed, had crossed the river during winter's low water and were now stuck on the other side, thanks to spring's runoff. So we tied his horse off to the bow of our dory, had the cowboy hop in, and ferried them across the river, the horse swimming and the cowboy high and dry.

The real fun began on the other side. We spent the next three hours trying to herd his cattle back across the river, using our kayaks as our steeds. The cowboy would round them up on his horse and Heeyaw! them into the water, then we'd peel out in our kayaks and nose them in the right direction, only to see them invariably swim and stampede back to the wrong shore. It was Billy Crystal's City Slickers, played out on the water.

Memories like these, stretched along the Yampa River's 250 miles from its birth in the Flat Tops Wilderness Area—which inspired Forest Service employee Arthur Carhart to champion today's wilderness preservation movement—to its confluence with the Green, are what hold the river as close to my heart as the cowboy's bandana was to his.

The Yampa is the last major free-flowing tributary to the Colorado, as unbridled as the wild horses in nearby Brown's Park, which once hosted Butch, Sundance and the Hole in the Wall Gang. It changes from a trickle in fall to a raging torrent in spring, cycling through every level in between.

Yet despite its pristine nature and natural hydrograph, not everything is honky-dory in Yampaland. It's also the last basin in the state with un-appropriated water.

With tunnels, pumpbacks and reservoirs already siphoning Western

Slope water to the growing Front Range, and drought-ridden states downstream clambering for more, there's a bounty on the Yampa's snowmelt. It faces threats from other users in the sun-drenched West, from Front Range municipalities to oil and mining operations. All this is prompting what could be a modern-day showdown at the Yampa Corral.

The demands on Colorado's water have prompted Colorado Governor John Hickenlooper to produce the state's first-ever water plan to better manage and protect our greatest resource. But the Yampa is squarely in the crosshairs. While the plan calls for protecting it, an elephant, or water buffalo, is in the room as well.

"The unanswered question is whether the Yampa will be tapped to meet the rest of the state's water needs," says Kent Vertrees, a member of the Yampa/White/Green River Roundtable, which recommends management plans for the basin. "It's likely not long before a trans-mountain diversion is proposed."

The Yampa has already fended off feuds for its lifeblood. In 2007, the Northern Colorado Water Conservancy District proposed a $4 billion Pumpback project that would've brought 20 percent of the river's high-water flow from Maybell to the Front Range, effectively de-watering the canyon's historic highs. Shell Oil filed for a water right to pump 8 percent of peak runoff into a 1,000-acre reservoir, introducing another player to the water table. The proposed Million Green River Pumpback project would pull water out of Flaming Gorge on the Green and deliver it to Greeley and Ft. Collins; this could lead to future calls for Yampa water.

"Keeping the Yampa wild is incredibly important," says Matt Rice of conservation group American Rivers. "It shows we can sustain vibrant agriculture while conserving endangered fish and supporting recreation."

Recreationally, the Yampa supports canoe, SUP and kayak schools, rafting operations, fishing concessions, and even a thriving tubing business exposing Triple Crown softball players to the river. It serves up a Class II-III town run whose C-hole was the basis for the city's Recreational Inchannel Diversion (RICD) water right, proving recreation is a "beneficial" use of the water; wildlife-lined floats through the Nature Conservancy's Carpenter Ranch; and wilderness sections through Class IV-V Cross Mountain Canyon—a 7-mile-long incision funneling the river's might into a chasm so fierce that ABC Sports once featured it on American Sportsmen—and iconic Yampa Canyon in Dinosaur National Monument. Float it and it's easy to see why late Sierra Club president David Brower fought so hard to save the river from the Echo Park Dam in 1956, marking one of the conservation world's most marquee victories.

The river also serves agricultural interests, two major coal mines, seven towns, snowmaking for the Steamboat Ski Resort and fulfills the state's water obligations to downstream users as outlined in the Colorado River's 1922 Water Compact. Its natural hydrograph supports such endangered species as the humpback chub *(Gila cypha),* bonytail *(G. elegans),* Colorado pikeminnow *(Ptychocheilus lucius),* and razorback sucker *(Xyrauchen texanus),* all endemic to the Yampa and reliant on its peak flows for spawning and nursery habitat. "Humpback Don't Want No Pumpback," local bumper stickers proclaim.

"The Yampa is an incredible resource," says Dinosaur National Monument Superintendent Mark Foust. "It preserves an amazing array of plant and animal communities along with the natural cycles they depend upon."

There's additional cavalry as well. In 2010, the BLM found three sections totaling 22 miles suitable for Wild & Scenic designation, including Williams Fork to Milk Creek, Milk Creek to Duffy Tunnel, and heralded Cross Mountain Canyon. And the best thing going for it is the state water plan, which recognizes the value of its free-flowing character.

Free-flowing character Peter VanDeCarr, owner of Steamboat's Backdoor Sports, also went to bat for it, in a more unorthodox way. In a case of vigilante justice that would do Charles Bronson proud, he spent 10 days kayaking the river from the town of Yampa near its headwaters all the way to Jensen, Utah. Instead of packing Bronson's heat, he packed a package of Hostess Twinkies inside a waterproof box. When he arrived in Jensen, he sold them to an outfitter for a quarter. "I wanted to show you can conduct inter-state commerce on it," he says. "That means it's navigable and land-owners can't block passage."

I was a Twinkies-eating, water droplet of man myself when I first rafted it on a five-day trip with my family in fifth grade. I remember kissing desert-varnish-striped Tiger Wall for good luck and giving my mom a bouquet of Indian Paintbrush, my face reddening like the flowers when a female guide saw the gesture.

A tighter bond formed when I moved just a block away from its banks in 1992. I paddle it and its tributaries, tube it with my daughters, soak in its riverside hot springs, swim in its pools, and cast blue-winged olives to its trout. The river even has its own river festival—complete with the world's first Crazy River Dog contest.

But the best memories come from longer courtship, namely floating the 71-mile Yampa Canyon run through Dinosaur National Monument. It's a tough permit to get: The success rate is just 6.6 percent—about the same as getting through Warm Springs rapid dry. But get one and you remember the trip for life. You pass outlaw hideouts, Indian ruins, pristine beaches and slot canyon hikes, while camping beneath desert stars and hearing guitars echo off the canyon walls.

Nowhere have I felt its essence more than sitting on a ridge once at camp when a lightning bolt burst through the heavens and sent a juniper into flames across the river. "Nice shot, Delaney!" yelled Drew, in reference to a kayaking friend who had recently died. We watched the flames spread throughout the night, fingers traveling underground through root lines and then popping up hundreds of yards away.

Then came the time I was subject to six riverside stitches on my pinkie from a dentist friend after I smashed it pounding in a horseshoe stake. I kayaked the whole river with it covered with gauze and a condom, sticking up like the digit of Austin Powers' Dr. Evil.

While Powers' alter-ego was after a million dollars, there are that many reasons why the river is dear to my heart, from deciphering its Fremont ruins and rock art to showing my daughters the cool magic of Whispering Cave and retracing John Wesley Powell's pioneering wake.

Like Powell and our hitchhiking cowboy, the river has seen its share of jams over the years, log and otherwise. But still it courses on, offering a valuable life lesson. And while it will likely face more threats in the future, as the region's wild stallions, outlaws and even a lone, free spirit like our cowboy know, there's infinite value in being wild and free.

Riding The Spike

Every sport has its Holy Grail, that pinnacle of perfect conditions. For surfers, it's catching a big swell. For skiers and snowboarders, that surprise 26-inch powder day. For fly fishers, perhaps that evasive cicada hatch, when any piece of foam lands a lunker. For kayakers, it's catching the Yampa River at peak flood, when the river is its biggest and baddest, boat-churning self.

It's one thing on a big snow year and you know it's coming. It's another when the runoff comes unexpectedly, as it did this week.
No one was holding out much hope for a decent high water year. But all that changed with a drop of the barometer. While everyone knew the rains were coming, no one thought it would lead to a record-setting spike for the date.

Forecasters called for a mid-week peak of 1,700 cubic feet per second (cfs). But the deluge brought down snow with it, causing the morning's flow report to read 2,900. It rose to 3,600 by early afternoon, and 4,000 shortly later, a high peak for even a big snow year.

And that's what brought out the big water dogs. They crawled out of the woodwork like telemark skiers emerging from the forest, congregating at the parking lot with grins as big as the river. People you hadn't seen all year were instantly back in your social circle as if no time had passed at all.

Of course, this also means there wasn't a lot of warm-up. For those who hadn't been in their boats yet, the season's first stroke led straight into the ligament-loosening Charlie's Hole. It was like hopping on a bronc cold turkey or road biking the 100-mile Gore Gruel off the couch. Dormant muscles and synapses were called into action pronto, taking a test they hadn't studied for. While this posed no problem for the youngsters, veterans' vertebrae voiced their concerns.

In a hydraulic like the C-hole, you take what it gives you. If you're a good boater, it's relatively benign. You're not going to get killed. Just thrashed. The worst-case scenario, aside from blowing out your shoulder, is missing your roll and swimming.

As with ocean surfing, the better you are the less severe the thrashing. Good surfers know how to duck-dive waves, avoid pearling and outsmart close-outs. Similarly, kayakers keep their elbows in a tight box to save their shoulders, know how and when to lean, and have their rolls as a backup. The better you are, the less you flip and chunder.

What's bad is getting exhausted during your ride and then flipping. Then you have to roll when you're whooped, oftentimes without a breath. Another bummer: sticking your roll, only to find you're still in the hole. Usually, when you flip you flush out and roll downstream. But sometimes the sticky part keeps you. You roll up to find yourself still in its clutches. The only solution: reaching down with your paddle blades in hopes the flowing water grabs them and pulls you out.

And all this is fun, in a shoulder-torturing, sadistic way. Onlookers might think you're crazy—and to a degree, you might be—but it looks worse than it is. It's a puzzle—figuring out how to surf the thing without getting pulverized. You lean back and edge your boat to avoid pearling and visiting Atlantis. If you're sideways, for the love of God, lean downstream so your upstream edge doesn't catch; if that happens you'll flip faster than a pancake at The Shack.

You multitask, balancing rudder pressure, side, forward and backward leans, stroke strength and cadence, and more. It's a hockey shift, Manic Training session and Lane of Pain bike climb all rolled into one. And you learn to stay away from the hole's far left side. That's the sticky, more munchy part.

If you're lucky, you'll emerge unscathed. You'll go in, bounce around, maybe try a few moves, and then get spit out like an orange seed. Conversely, you'll get throttled, rolling up with water coming out of every unprotected orifice.

How good is it when it's big? Enough that former world kayak freestyle champions Nick Troutman and Emily Jackson often swing through town in their RV, with son Tucker in tow, to practice between competitions.

Alas, this kind of runoff means it'll be over quickly. But like a ski year, you remember the highs more than the lows. So you rally while it's there and mow the lawn later. The honey-do list will still be on the fridge in July; not so the high water. Your shoulders just have to outlast the snowmelt.

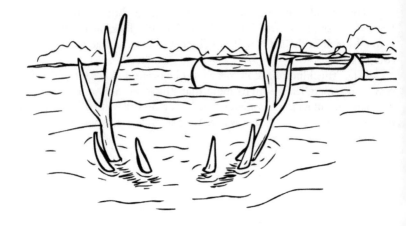

Supping for Shed Antlers

We've all had those times when something Colorado-ish just clicks—a moonrise over the aspen, a rainbow framing a deer, a trout rise in the early morning mist. My mile-high moment came when even the good lord above would've had a hard time scripting a more scenic scenario from our 38th state.

It came while floating the Carpenter Ranch stretch of the Yampa near Hayden. I knew as soon as we put on in our collective craft—a motley hodgepodge of canoes, sit-on-tops, inflatable kayaks, tubes and stand-up paddleboards, carrying 16 people, from toddlers to grandparents—that we were in for a treat.

Temperatures were topping 90 degrees in town, the river was cool and clear, and the level and difficulty were well within range of my 80-year-old mom propelling herself in a solo inflatable. (Excluding when she asked, "Which way are we going?" as soon as we put in. Answer: downstream.)

Rounding a bend on my paddleboard, we spied a nice, sandy beach for lunch and bee-lined for it. As I paddled into the eddy, I happened to glance down from my higher-than-normal-paddlecraft perch and eyed what at first looked like a bunch of sticks protruding up from the sandy bottom, about three feet below the surface.

As the current whisked me by, it became as clear as the water that it was a full elk antler rack, buried in water but prongs pointing skyward toward the heavens and catching errant rays of sunlight filtering through the golden water. But then I was past it and they were gone.

"Holy antlers in Atlantis!" I mustered, quickly sizing up a bush on shore as a reference point from which to line up a search. As soon as we beached our craft, we grabbed our snorkel masks (yes, we brought those, too) and fanned out to find the sunken prize.

Combing the area in question, forming an avalanche transceiver-type grid pattern in the waist- to shoulder-deep water, we came up empty until we heard a piercing cry from 11-year-old Emily.

"I found them!" she shouted, diving under with her mask.

We all quickly scurried over, pulling it up out of the water. Lo and behold, it was a full five-by-five elk antler rack complete with half a skull, meaning it wasn't a shed. Drips plopped off each point into the river in cadence with their size.

We then carried it to shore, where we posed with it and eventually mounted it to the front of our canoe as a figurehead for the rest of the trip. It was in the middle of all of this that we turned to see Chuck paddle up on his paddleboard, showcasing another icon of Colorado: a 20-inch rainbow trout on the end of his fishing line. Through the antler's framework on the prow of our canoe, I saw him play it and land it, his rod arcing with the grace of a gymnast's backbend.

And Colorado's calling card wasn't through. Just then, we turned our heads skyward to see a bald eagle swoop by, paralleling the river with a small bird in its talons and the prey's mother giving chase. It was a hat-trick even Thoreau or Muir would have a hard time topping.

It all happened at about the same time—antlers, trout and eagle—rendering us with Centennial State Sensory Overload Syndrome (CSSOS), an affliction we were more than willing to endure as we cracked our Coors on shore.

Of course, as a Broncos' orange and blue sunset covered the sky on the float out, the antlers casting a lattice of shadows along the canoe, we also bore witness to one of Colorado's other seasonal wonders that too often comes with the territory: mosquitoes.

Nothing in life, it seems—even those quintessential Colorado moments—comes free.

Trout Maestro

As conductor of the Omaha and Steamboat Springs Symphony orchestras, Ernest Richardson is used to waving his batons around. But examine the tips of his custom music sticks and another passion surfaces involving swinging a rod over a stream instead of over a symphony.

Inlaid into each baton tip are his two favorite flies for Steamboat's Yampa River, which he fishes every time he comes to town: a Rusty spinner and chartreuse midge pupa. "That's what I use every time I come here," says Richardson, who got his first fly rod—a nine-foot, six-weight Fisher Original, which he still has—while vacationing in nearby Fraser after college. "I use the Rusty in the evening on the town stretch, and the pupa on the Stagecoach tail waters."

The fishing bug bit Richardson when he was 10 and saw three lake trout in his hometown of Heber Springs, Arkansas. "From that point forward I knew I wanted to catch fish," he says.

But before chasing rainbows, he chased bowed instruments. Playing since he was 3, he began his formal string education at Indiana University under Tadeusz Wronski, before concentrating on the viola, and later, composition and conducting, at the University of Michigan. He began his conducting career with the Phoenix Symphony Orchestra, before taking over the Omaha Symphony Orchestra in 1992. If that's not enough, he also holds a black belt in tae kwon do.

As the 20-year resident conductor of the Omaha Symphony, he fishes the local lakes for bass, panfish, crappies and blue gill, and even the occasional unorthodox species. "Oddly enough, I once caught a catfish on a surface fly," he says. "I thought it was a big bass until I saw it circling." When his career brings him to northwest Colorado, he eyes his baton tips. "I fish the Yampa every time I come out, no matter the season," he says.

Nowhere did his two passions merge better than when he recently conducted "A River Runs Through It," whose overtures by Beethoven and Vivaldi were accompanied by projected river photographs by John Fielder.

As for similarities between casting his fly rod and swinging his batons, he says it depends on the music. "If the music is broad and sweeping, you don't use much wrist," he says. "But if it's fast and percussive, it's all wrist. But I don't use wrist motion casting—I'm not advanced enough for that yet."

Getting in the zone of each, he adds, is also similar. "Both the music and water compel your gestures," he says. "In music, we use patterns but don't plan out our gestures. It's the same on rivers. When I'm in the zone fly fishing, as opposed to hooking trees and the occasional chipmunk, I don't think about the cast. I just look where the fly needs to be. Then, when I actually catch a fish, that's the music."

He equates building his own batons to tying flies. "It's the same feeling," he says. "It gives you a more personal connection to what you're doing."

For him, tying flies is easier, since conducting comes more naturally than carpentry. "I was doing a home project in Omaha and I made four pine balusters and screwed up all of them," he says. "So I thought I could turn them into conducting batons."

But it was hard, he adds, because, like a fly rod, a baton has to have the right feel. "The handle has to weigh the exact same as the stick so it's balanced," he says. His solution: filling the batons' hollow cores with fishing split shot and squirting in leftover epoxy. That same epoxy spawned the idea to shellac his two favorite Rocky Mountain flies to the ends.

"I showed them to a colleague who looked at me like I was crazy," he says. "But then I saw a slight conductor indie thing in his eye. I think he wanted one."

Still don't think he's a virtuoso at both disciplines? Consider his email prefix: trout-maestro.

L · A · N · D

A Seasonal Two-fer

Recreational overlaps come with the territory in mountain towns. At one point last spring, too lazy to shuffle things off, my schizophrenic ski rack held a snowboard, hockey stick, kayak paddle and fly rod, with my bike in the next rack over.

But now it's September, and two of the items, my bike and fly rod, haven't seen enough use. The solution: Use them both on the same outing. With mountain biking and mayflies about to be trounced by winter, it was time to double dip (while scorned with chips at parties, it works whenever Mother Nature's staring you down).

Doing so takes logistics—you have to remember the Hare's Ear and helmet—as well as coordination. In the old days I'd stuff my two-piece rod inside a PVC pipe duct-taped to my cross bar. It'd hang over my front wheel like a battering ram, threatening trees on every corner and chafing my inside leg with every pedal (try explaining those bruises to your spouse).

The good news about my daughter dislodging my rod from our raft on a recent river trip was that it led to my Alaskan brother-in-law building me a new four-piece one, complete with inlaid Grateful Dead dancing bears and a skull-and-crossbones end cap. Now the pedal-with-pole spaz-factor has ebbed; I simply stash its four pieces in a pack. More importantly, this new streamlined technique doesn't broadcast to everyone that I'm biking into a secret fishing spot. While mountain bikers aren't overly territorial ("Duude, that's my dirt"), fishermen are; exposing a fishing stash is worse than doing so for a powder stash.

So I'll disguise my dual-sport locale. Suffice it to say that it involves a pass named after bison that offers a trail down to a creek named after a carbonated beverage (I'll mention Mountain Dew to throw you off track).

Hit it in the fall and that's what you get: red and gold aspen leaves sticking to your tires from glistening condensation. The kaleidoscope of colors mesmerizes you with every tire rotation. You have to remember to look up from tire and trail to dodge errant obstacles. While the ride itself is rewarding, at its end comes the clencher; that's when you break out your rod.

A relatively lame fly fisher, I'm a creature of habit. But here it works; I always tie on the smallest Royal Coachman in my antiquated arsenal. I like the Coachman not because the fish can see it, but because I can. It makes me feel better. Not in the "I'm okay and people like me" sense, but because I can see if it's leaving contrails like a jetliner or is floating drag-free. If it's the former, I pick it up and sling it again until it becomes one with the flow, just like fall absorbing summer.

The creek bed is tight, lined with bushes, trees and curse-word-causing branches. With a nine-foot rod, back casts have no room for error. More than once I grovel to the bank to release my precious Coachman from a wayward limb.

Then it's back to casting, my fly falling between wisps of mist rising from trickle-fed pools. Tantalizing whatever mouths wait below, it hovers, occasionally spinning like the wheels of the bike that brought me here. Then Bam! (or maybe a small bam!) a strike, a hook set, and a brookie is fooled into a brief visit to the atmosphere. I let it go, and then catch several more from the same pool before they wise up. When they do, I head upstream and start all over again. A cast and another strike. The fish are all small, tiny in fact, but I don't care. I'm not here for the fight or trophy. I have fun with six inches skiing, and I do here as well.

When the shadows grow longer than my casts, and the cold numbs my fingers into clubs, I wade back downstream to my dual-suspension steed. Then I break down my rod, stuff it in my pack and begin the pedal home. On the way I think of another spot to possibly hit before the garage reclaims two more pieces of gear. It's off a road named after wapiti, with a trail offering vistas of snow-capped peaks by a series of beaver ponds pock-marked by rises. Perhaps I just might be able to squeeze in another twofer before the snow flies…

Blade Runner

I'll admit it...I'm not much of a runner—unless I'm being chased, which happens far less than it used to. I'm happy expanding my lung capillaries through less cartilage-pounding pursuits.

This comes despite having Olympic marathon runner Frank Shorter living in our basement apartment in Boulder when he won the Games in 1972. He called our house the night he won, invited us on the first mile or so of his training runs and, most importantly, gave us the green light to raid his barrels of GORP.

But since then, my penchant for jogging has worn as thin as a well-used sneaker sole. I'd rather save whatever shreds of cartilage I have left for more fun pursuits, like powder skiing and mountain biking. That said, spring is the one time of the year I'll strap on the Nikes; when there's too little snow to ski and the trails are too muddy to ride. And I'm not the only one. A week ago my friend Peter got caught jogging in a rainstorm, bemoaning, "And I don't even run!"

But here's why I like it this time of year:

Once the snow melts, the grass is matted down like wet dog hair after a romp in the Yampa. This means you can go anywhere; you're not restricted to the trail. It's like crust skiing on skate skis, only you're running. Perhaps call it bent-blade running?

One foray took me up Emerald meadows, where the grass was as packed down as Woodstock's fields. Free from trail restraints, I zig-zagged up the hill to stop my heart from doing so, and eventually made it to the field's top, where fingers of land continued upward between receding snow patches. Fly a drone and it'd look like a giant hand giving a high five. So I did little mini-intervals up and down each snow-bordered finger, ignoring the sponges on my feet getting soggier each stride.

The middle finger proved the day's elevation highpoint, and after the pinkie I turned around and bounded back down, springing off the rubbery grass as if I was wearing springs.

On a later outing, I followed up our local creek, which was pumping as fast as my pulse. Again forsaking the trail, I followed it up directísmo, fording it countless times. Bush blocking my way? Jump over the creek and head left. Branch about to shish-kebob my eyeball? Hop to the opposite soggy bank. And often came the inevitable hunched-over bush grovel, all while technically still "running."

The main benefit of these creeks, of course, is the distraction they provide. They give you something else to think about besides the lung you're coughing up. And their gurgling overrides your breathing. You can space out on the babbling water and then, voila!, you've knocked off another quarter mile as easily as wolfing down a Quarter Pounder.

Near the creek's top, I followed the great Yogi Berra's advice: If you see a fork in the road, take it. So I headed off to the right, and was soon running alongside a ribbon of waterfalls through a verdant field flanked by yellow buttercups. It took all my will not to hum the Sound of Music.

Later, the hills literally were alive as I hopped, like a giant doing hurdles, over a maze of vole tunnels crisscrossing the countryside. Like the dirt-moving voles, early season running also lets you unearth history. Veering from the field back into the forest, I stumbled upon the remains of an old dairy farm foundation, standing proud before being reclaimed by resident grasses and ferns. Buried the rest of the year by snow or undergrowth, it was now exposed, letting those of us foolish and footloose enough to find it play resident archaeologist.

Combine this go-anywhere, flattened-down grass with birds singing, trees budding, flowers blooming and creeks gurgling, and you can see why running, for me at least, gains steam in the mud-season—even if I run out of it faster than Frank.

Bridging the Seasons

Am I the only one to do this? Every fall riding the bike path, I start slaloming around leaves as if I'm running gates on the ski slopes. I veer this way and that, angling into turns and carving around whatever has fallen from the heavens like a veritable Lindsey Vonn vadeling down the Core Trail.

Not that I'm a racer. Far from it. All I have under my notched-on-the-last-hole belt are a few ski patrol races from my college days and cellar-dweller finishes in the local Town Challenge series (rec division, if you must know).

But for some reason, plying my inner Bode Miller on the bike path comes as naturally as my thoughts about the upcoming ski season. People might mutter "doofus" at my derring-do, but so be it; it's my way of bridging the seasons in Steamboat.

While sticks, stones and any other markings are all fair game, the real gates, and best harbingers of the coming winter, are the leaves. I'll be turning wide and loose and then all of a sudden—leaf, leaf, leaf!—a flush of foliage sends my handlebars weaving.

As fall progresses, more leaves flutter down, meaning more gates. September's SuperG progresses to a GS and finally a quick-turning slalom come October.

So I'm ripe for a shrink. The ritual is a sign that the season itself is shrinking and winter is on its way.

Of course, more obvious omens exist as well, from the sprinkler guy coming to blow out your lines to the size of skunk cabbage and the fuzziness of caterpillars. It can even be found in the football games blaring from bar TVs along Yampa Avenue. They all mean Old Man Winter is coming out of his slumber.

Such recreational overlaps come with the territory here, no matter what side of the equinox we're on. And it's these bridge seasons—when your golf bag, fly rod, bike and skate skis all jockey for position in your car—that make living here so great.

Of course, sometimes I get carried away, like when I find myself slalom-walking around leaves, which isn't nearly as fun. And let me know if you ever see me weaving the cart down the grocery aisle...then I'll know I have a problem.

Ski Bikes!

Another sign of seasonal bridgedom? Ski bikes.

Steamboat has an ongoing rivalry between the nicknames Ski Town USA and Bike Town USA. If local Josh Westfall has his way, we'd be known as Ski Bike Town USA.

Type II ski bikes—not to be confused with the Type I snow bikes the resort rents, where riders wear mini-skis on each foot—are gaining traction, thanks to Westfall's line of Lenz Sport ski bikes.

With short skis fore and aft in place of wheels, the bikes employ up to eight inches of full-suspension travel, "turning a four-inch powder day into a 12-inch powder day," Westfall says. "They have the same suspension as downhill mountain bikes. They go anywhere."

Indeed, Westfall and his followers have taken them down nearly every run at Steamboat, including the Chutes and into the backcountry of Fish Creek. Last year, he got 50 days in on them.

Still, he admits adoption has been slow. "It's still too new for mainstream acceptance," he says. "Resorts aren't quite sure what to do with them yet."

Joining Steamboat and Vail in allowing them is Purgatory and Winter Park (which even hosts biker cross and park events). In Steamboat, they're held to the same rules as skis or snowboards, but not allowed in any park. The sport's website (www.ski-bike.org) lists resorts allowing them as well as events, including New Mexico's annual Sipapu Ski-bike Rally, the Purgatory Ski-bike Festival and Hoodoo Mountain, Oregon's Spring Fling.

Their cult-like following stems from their fun factor. "It's great for us old guys," says Westfall's dad, Don, 65, who's coming off knee surgery. "It's way easier on your body than skiing or snowboarding."

Their learning curve, adds Westfall, is quicker and less painful than snowboarding, which I discovered quickly. There are three keys: keep your chin over the crossbar while standing on the pegs; keep your weight on the uphill footpeg when turning, bending your elbows outward and standing bowl-legged; and "buttering" your turns to scrub speed, which is the only way to slow down. After an hour we were onto the blues and there was one more convert to the craze.

"It's like mountain biking, but you can go anywhere it's white," says local Aryeh Copa, a lifelong skier and mountain biker. "It's mountain biking with choices you never had before."

"It's a completely different sport than the ones with tiny foot-skis," adds Westfall. "It's part mountain biking, skiing, snowboarding, dirt biking and snowmobiling—a total Colorado sport. It belongs in the X Games."

And yes, on my last run I saw a leaf to turn around.

Channeling My Inner Tarahumara

Blame it on the Tarahumara. Or author Christopher McDougall and his cryptic character Caballo Blanco.

How else would you explain the harebrained idea of hopping off the couch to jog the Zirkle Circle, an 11-mile, 2,400-vertical loop in the Mount Zirkle Wilderness Area connecting Gilpin and Gold Creek lakes?

It wouldn't be so bad if I were actually a runner, those sadists who pound the pavement a few times each week. But I'm not. I got one run in all summer, a pathetic attempt to keep up with my 17-year-old daughter on a paltry three-miler.

I'm halfway through McDougall's book, "Born to Run," about the barefoot-bounding Tarahumara Indians of Mexico's Copper Canyon. With callouses as honed as their cardio, they regularly open a royal can of whoop-ass on Nike-footed ultra runners in such stateside events as the Leadville 100. They've even shown their toes at Steamboat's own Run Rabbit Run 100-miler.

So, inspired by their antics and my own Doritos-eating slouchdom, I decided to walk in their shoes—or rather, run—even if they often do so barefoot. How hard could it be to whip off 11 miles?

After filling the kids' cereal bowls and shooing them off to school, I filled my hydration pack, threw in a raincoat and some Honey Stinger chews and drove north to the Slovenia trailhead. I hedged my bet—and heart rate— by planning to fly-fish a high alpine meadow halfway through, throwing my rod and four flies in my pack (I didn't want the weight of a fifth).

If fishing en route broke with Tarahumara tradition, so did my shoes: a pair of 16-year-old Nikes, whose foam is as compressed as my 53-year-old vertebrae. I wasn't about to take the beat-down barefoot.

The gaggle of other hikers at the trailhead had dispersed by the time I gazelled out of the gate at 9:07 a.m., taking the route clockwise. And then I jogged off into the great, blistering unknown.

Technically, I can use the term jogging, defined as "running at a steady gentle pace, especially on a regular basis as a form of physical exercise." The "regular basis" part didn't apply, but I was certainly going at a gentle pace. Another definition calls jogging "running slower than 6 mph; distinguished from running by wider lateral foot-strike spacing, adding stability at slower speeds or when coordination is lacking." My little shuffle steps were half that speed, and my lack of coordination surfaced at my first stumble: catching a rock right off the bat from not lifting my toe high enough.

A quarter-mile in, the registration kiosk saved me; might as well fill it out, I reasoned, and write down my next of kin. My next barometer of progress was the sign marking the turn-off to Mica Lake; it seemed a lot farther than I remembered.

Plodding on, I banked some karma at a creek crossing. Two women were wondering which way to go and I showed them, pointing without even breaking stride. And since they saw me running, I had to keep running.

I'd planned on taking my first break at Gilpin Lake. But I kept going, counting wind-chop breaks to break up the tedium. Eventually, I passed a group of eight in jeans, and soon five others near the top of the ridge. Exchanging pleasantries, one asked if I was a Christian and said I could join them in a group mass when the rest of their party arrived. Having enough foot pain already without thinking about crucifixions, I politely declined. Besides, I had fish—and my breath—to catch.

On the way down, I passed their other religious runners coming up the opposite way, several reciting the Lord's prayer. Had I joined in, I'd have replaced Our Father with Our Faciiitis. Like the Tarahumara, one runner was even barefoot—a tortuous way to "forgive us our trespasses."

After 20 minutes or so, I hit the meadow and broke out my fly rod. Total time without stopping: two and a half hours. Whoa...hadn't done anything like that in a long time. While I only caught one fish, at one point taking off my shoes Tarahumara-style to ford the creek, the bigger reward was the break.

It was all downhill from there, paralleling a creek to Gold Creek Lake and then following a rock-filled trail down to the valley bottom. I calculated that if each Honey Stinger chew took a quarter-mile to suck, eight of the morsels would last two miles. En route, I passed hikers heading down and backpackers heading up, my inner Tarahumara Indian on full display. I even passed a white horse coming up, perhaps the specter of the book's Caballo Blanco or maybe just a hallucination from my hypoxia.

Eventually, I jogged it back to the kiosk junction and final stretch home—not exactly a horse returning to the barn, but I could sense the end was near. Back at my car, my watch read 2:07 p.m.—about five hours total. But an hour ten was spent fishing and another ten untangling my line, so that meant 3:40 of running. Halfway respectable, until realizing the fastest marathon was run in 2:03—at two and a half times the distance.

Still, I was happy—at least until I shoe-horned myself out of the car and limped into the Clark Store for some chocolate milk, knowing my daughter's soccer coach recommends it for recovery. That's when my ankles, calves and knees rebelled, letting out their own Tarahumara war cry. But at least I have one thing the Tarahumara don't: a hot tub waiting back home.

Free Summer Concert Series Kudos

Come summertime in Steamboat, the Free Summer Concert Series is the best thing going. Here's why:

It's free. There are no tickets to worry about, and no fretting over if you can afford it. Just good old free music, like it's supposed to be.

The access. You can get to it by foot, bike, tube, rollerblades or even One Wheel. Nordic skiers could even arrive after flying off the Nordic jump and landing on its turf. I like walking to it from my house in Fairview, pre-gaming as we go.

Because you bump into people. Like Scott Fox, who spreads the rumor that Robert Plant is in town and might come on to play with the Chris Robinson Brotherhood. Or Kent Vertrees, who has a stranger in tow he just met up on Buff Pass who's horseback-delivering horses to Bozeman, but was convinced to come into town for the night. He hadn't seen a person for days and is now front row, as bewildered as a deer in the headlights.

Because you bump into more people. Some people you end up talking to longer than you'd like, and others not long enough. The key: keep moving. That's how you see friends you haven't seen for ages.

Because of the VIP tent. Buy a pass for the season and you get beer, food and a great place to hang.

Because there's no better way to cap a bluebird Colorado day. I can only imagine what it's like being on stage playing to such a scene.

Because of the line-up. Nice work, booking committee. It's not easy getting top-notch acts to come to the boonies of Northwest Colorado, but every year the music gets better and better. Musicians from the Black Crows, Neville Brothers and Radiators? Now wave your hand in the air and give me an "oooh ya" for Ziggy Marley.

Because of the setting. You're at the base of five different Nordic jumps. Where else has that? Then take your eyes off the stage and look at the circle of mountains around you. Not a bad view at all.

Because of the beer. Nice addition, organizers, having two-for-one happy hour brewhas from 5:30-6:30 pm.

Because of the after-gigs. Anyone else go to the livestream of the Grateful Dead show at the Chief after the New Orleans Suspects show? Or Hot Buttered Rum at Schmiggity's? What's not to like?

Because of the Hula Hoops. Seriously? Can girls really gyrate that well with a round piece of glow-in-the-dark plastic around their bodies? (The glow-hoops retail for $500.)

Because of the rodeo. Yup, pardners. While you're reveling in music, just a Frisbee's toss away some of the best cowboys in the country are riding broncs and bulls to the ringside announcing of John Shipley. How Americana can you get?

Because of its family-friendliness. Go ahead, bring the whole gang. Establish a base camp with a blanket and then let them run around. Sometimes there's even bubble and birdseed baths in the back.

Because of the front row. You have to get up there for at least a few minutes every show. It lets you see the musicians up close, unleash your inner groupie and bump into even more people you know before returning back to the kids. Sure, it's a little awkward when you bump into your teenage daughter, but what the hey? Plus, it's good practice for working your way through a real crowd.

The Garden State

The state of our garden at home could be likened to that of the administration of Garden State Governor Steve Christie: relative disarray. Only where Christie is battling traffic jam scandals, we're battling a traffic jam of weeds.

Neither our lawn nor flower bed would make the cover of Gardening magazine. The lawn's good enough for donning a white shirt and mint julep for an occasional game of croquet, and for kicking the soccer ball with the kids, but that's about it. Last year marked the first time I fertilized it in years; the year before, the inaugural rental of one of those hole-punching gizmos that leaves those dog-turd cylinders all around. For a while its greenest patch was where I spilled trim stain on it, until even that blob browned. Every year, mini-grasshoppers munch it down more than our mower.

Speaking of which, that's in equal disrepair. It's a $50 jobber that I actually, for some reason, drove over the Continental Divide from the Front Range—likely the cheapest mower to ever have that honor. It should be in the Smithsonian for the fact that it still runs. I can't remember the last time I sharpened the blades or changed the oil, and it has more bailing-wire than factory-installed cables. A twisted piece of wire jerry-rigs the broken throttle spring so it's on max all the time, the starter rope has more knots than threads, and the grass chute, which falls off from errant bumps, is held on by a stripped Phillips-head screw. But even without OSHA certification, it runs on three-year-old gasoline well enough to shred UV-deteriorated trampoline padding to smithereens.

Then comes our flower "garden." Despite its brilliant, hand-placed stonework with stair-stepped beds, which I built one summer as self-assigned ACL rehab, it, too, is in shambles. Its sprinkler system Old Faithfuls on one corner from a broken head, and it harbors more grass than geraniums. A tree that was once a mere sapling now wedges a retaining rock onto the lawn every year, its stone staircase-to-nowhere leads straight into a bush, and we have the world's only lilac that never flowers.

It's a miracle we get perennial blooms at all, even though just up the trail on Emerald Mountain flowers do great in the wild. A handful of lupine refuse to die no matter how hard I try, a rose bush brandishes more thorns than buds, and delinquent daisies crowd everything else out like Mafioso owning the place. Since they're our only real flowers, I never bother to rein them in.

It's dismal and disheveled, compared to what it could be, but I have a feeling that this year things are going to be a little different around the old Buchanan homestead. I plan to make our garden and lawn better than ever...as soon as I get back from my mountain bike ride.

Movement of Ja People

Bob Marley would be proud of Steamboat. Every spring break there's an exodus, a movement of the people as locals abandon mud season for greener and warmer pastures. And this year more than most, it seems that movement was to Moab.

Yep, that Utah Mecca for all things desert, including mountain biking, canyon hiking, Milt burgers and 3.2 percent beer from Eddy McStiff's to bloat you afterward. Seems you couldn't swing a dead cat this year and not hit someone from Steamboat.

Certainly, there are other hot spots luring locals away from wearing galoshes in a ghost town. Places like Costa Rica, the Yucatan, Nuevo Vallarta and California regularly draw crowds away from all mountain towns come the Big Thaw. But if you were to bet on a single city claiming the most visitors from our own local zip code (80477) this year, put your money on Moab.

Maybe it's the economy that caused locals to forsake that trip to the Seychelles or Bonaire this year. Maybe it's the fact that the ski season plain sucked, dishing up temps that reminded everyone of scorpions, sand and cacti. Maybe it's the fact that national parks were free as part of National Get Outdoors Week. And maybe it's the fact that Moab is simply a magnet for like-minded people who appreciate the outdoors. Whatever it is, this year saw a Steamboat-to-sandstone pilgrimage like no other.

I know because we were among the Routt County ranks making the migration. I saw more people on Slickrock than I do at City Market. Mill Creek Falls might as well have been the Old Town Hot Springs. San Miguel's might have been that favorite local's bar, Sun Pies. Corona Arch? Might as well have been sipping Coronas at Carl's.

We were spared the majority of Steamboat Does Moab. We didn't arrive until Wednesday night, five days after break started, waylaid first by a river trip on the San Juan and afterward by a quick jaunt to Mesa Verde.

But once we arrived, it was as social a scene as our local summer concert series. First stop: filling up our water jug at the a friend's household, who were hosting a happy hour reminiscent of any back home. Represented were five families from Routt County. From there, we headed to our campsite at Sand Flats, where several other Steamboat families had already taken up residence, including the Starkey's, Hobsons, Franklins, Wallisches, Millers, Birkinbines, Bonifaces, Weibels and Skovs.

The next day saw us hike to Corona Arch, Moab's version of Fish Creek Falls, where we bumped into the Smiths. During an afternoon squall, we found shelter (and welcome showers) at the rec center, where we ran into Cafe Diva's Daryl Newcomb, also washing off the sand. He, too, was camping at Sand Flats with several other Steamboaters not on above said list.

Later, after dishing our daughter and her friend off at a "sleepover" at a house rented by the Musselmans, we returned to our site only to see that the Flanigans had moved in.

We remained relatively Steamboat-free during the next day's activities, including mountain bike rides on the Intrepid and Bar M trails, until that night when we bumped into the Rosemonds on Main Street, fresh back from four-wheeling in the Needles.

We managed a Routt County reprieve with a slot canyon hike near Goblin Valley on our way home, but it was short lived. Over our backyard fence neighbor Newton mentioned that he had just returned from Moab with the entire Nordic team. The next day I found that our friends the Frithsens and Gambers had also put Moab on their map.

That's more than 20 different bloodlines from the 'Boat, and that's just from our saddled-with-kids social circle. Countless more invariably slipped through the desert, census cracks. For the week I'd venture that no other town was better represented in Desert Town USA than Ski Town USA.

I couldn't even escape it on the final day of break when I went out to ride the just-opened trails of Emerald Mountain. What trail did I find myself on after taking in the view from the Quarry? Steamboat Moab...

Riding New Trails

Call it pressing glass for pedalers.

That was the buzz recently as, while town's more cardio-oriented raced the 50-mile Stinger Challenge, the more mortally lunged among us ogled 4.25-mile Morning Gloria, town's newest mountain bike trail.

It's a lot like the old rope drop on the mountain, where you had to wait for ski patrollers to drop the rope at the top of the gondola to ski the fresh turns beyond. You knew the goods were there, but you had to wait for permission. Morning Gloria was there ready to ride as well, but a closed sign prohibited access. Until word got out that it was officially open.

For mountain bikers, riding a new trail is like skiers schussing a new mountain, paddlers navigating a new canyon, or fishermen casting a new waterway. And when it happens in your backyard, it's even better.

The chance doesn't come often. Most trails around Steamboat have been here since before disc brakes; the last new cross-country trail of this magnitude was the Beall Trail in 2010. Riding a new one usually means hitting some super remote, mosquito-festered, hike-a-bike or driving somewhere. This one's out our backdoor.

That it was built so quickly—two months, to be exact—owes itself to the ability of Routt Country Rider's new $100,000, root-eating, trail-building machine. And while the building of some of town's other new trails had been done rather secretively, the cat was out of the bag early for Morning Gloria, amping up anticipation.

Apart from trail workers assessing their handiwork and errant poachers, the jury's out on who "officially" rode it first. While it opened last Friday, my chance, being the hard-working father figure that I am, didn't come until Tuesday, four days after its ribbon cutting. For bragging rights, that's like hitting the gondo at noon on a powder day.

Still, while I might not have gotten "first tracks," my eyes widened like the trail's three-foot width as I veered off Lupine and onto terra incognito, a veritable Livingstone exploring the Nile. Each crank of the pedal brought something new, from arching scrub oak caverns to platoons of pine trees and fern-filled aspen groves.

Because I knew no one else had named them yet, I bestowed certain sections with such monikers as Beetle Kill Trees, Goblin Forest, Valley View Turn, Tree Coin Stack Straight-away, Twisted Aspen, Nose Blow Corner and Elk Track Narrows.

Around one corner I came upon trail builders Marc and Gretchen Sehler, putting a few finishing touches on a turn. I was the first to clean it, they said, since their most recent shovel work.

And I ran into several other locals out doing the exact same thing on their lunch break, all with similar expressions of exploration. We were like kids in a riding version of the Rocket Fizz candy store.

Tidbit of note: the trail has 35 switchbacks, or one for every 0.12 miles (yes, I counted). That's far more than the six going up Blackmere Drive, the four up Quarry Mountain or the big fat zero up the Lane of Pain. But they maintain a quad-friendly gradient that make it the easiest way up to the top.

Flag firmly planted on the summit up top at the junction of Quarry Mountain and Root Canal, I turned around and rode back, exploring it with the help of gravity. It rides down just as well, from a width allowing for diplomatic yielding to banked turns that leave your wheels spinning and mouth grinning.

Soon I was back in the office, my excuse to blow out of work gone in the dust. They say you only get one chance to make a first impression and Morning Gloria nailed it in spades—the same ones its builders used to polish its path. But let me think...was it actually 35 switchbacks? I might just have to head back for a little more reconnaissance.

Riding the Moots Ranch Rally

You ever notice that ouch is part of "off the couch?"

I did this weekend, when joining local bike manufacturer Moots on its annual, 50-mile Moots Ranch Rally, a communal dirt-road ride showcasing area ranches while benefitting the Community Agriculture Alliance.

Showing up at their headquarters Saturday morning, my baggy shorts stuck out from the lycra-clad as much as my fitness did. My ace up my sleeve was my ride: a borrowed-from-Moots, 18-lb., Vamoots DR, complete with disk brakes and electronic shifters that switched gears better than my car.

That I got it sized at the last minute spelled more good news: After imbibing coffee and pastries, the main group took off at the buzzer, meaning I didn't have to suffer the indignity of getting passed. I was off the back from the get-go, which suited my style just fine. Not that it mattered; the ride was billed as "non-competitive," drawing everyone from Olympians and World Champions like Ruthie Matthes to regular shift-down-when-you-meant-to-shift-up Joes like me.

With that we were off, Moots president Butch Boucher graciously starting out with said media attendee. With the pack well ahead, we spun up Routt County Road 129 and then turned left onto RCR 44 and ranchville. From here, it got a bit confusing, the route filled with road name variations of 44-E, -A and -Ds as well as 46, 52, 54 and 56-somethings. I should have left a trail of bread crumbs if I hoped to follow it again. Suffice it to say it took us across the Elk River and around a jollier and greener-than-ever Sleeping Giant, past creeks I never knew existed and ranches I never knew were there.

Which, of course, was the whole point. When my head wasn't down and heart in my throat, I'd see such ranches as Sherrod, Soash Farm, Monger, Belton, Wolf Mountain, Smith Rancho, Fait Haystack, Long

Gulch and other icons of Steamboat's Western heritage whiz by. One, I kid you not, was even named Werdaphucawee (please pronounce out loud). In their busiest time of year, all were more practical than pretentious; some small, some big, some with long honey-do lists and some immaculate. But they all shared a vital cog to our colorful past.

According to a recent USDA Ag Census, they're part of 799 Routt County farms and ranches whose annual agriculture sales exceed $46 million. That's a lot of dough for an under-appreciated aspect of the local economy lost in today's tourism-oriented era—especially one that was here way before Honey Stinger and GoPros.

Dusted by my wingmen, eventually I made it to the aid station at mile 25, where my buddies were waiting (I told them that I stopped to help a trio of gals fix a flat, but I don't think they believed me). It was oddly fitting, I noted, that we had to pass the Deep Creek cemetery to get here.

Fueled and "rested," it was then off on another set of numerically alphabetized roads before the brief pavement of C.R. 129 led back to 54 to 52-E. Or was it 52 to 54-E? Whatever, it led to a final climb up Fly Gulch, where I actually saw a silver fork lying in the road; with apologies to Yogi Berra, I didn't stop to take it.

This all led back to 44, where we—my new slower rider buddies and I—rode to lunch at the Rocking C Bar Ranch, owned by Doc and Marsha Daughenbaugh. Cowhands and kids sprayed a cow's derriere in a stall as we ate sandwiches from Backcountry Deli under the shade of a giant, multi-limbed cottonwood tree.

"It was a great event, with perfect weather," maintains Marsha, who in her spare time heads the CAA. "It took riders past some of the area's classic ranches and offered spectacular views. Everyone seemed to appreciate our ranching heritage."

While I certainly did, I also appreciated that the end was near. A few miles later, after 50 miles and 2,600 vertical feet (about 50 feet per mile, but who's counting?), the ride ended with a party at the Moots factory with beer by Butcherknife, food by Drunken Onion and, later, a quad massage by my wife. While I might not have been first out of the gate at the start, you should have seen me sprint for the keg.

The Sage Grouse Strut: A Lesson in Love

I might be a little better at that "I don't wanna be a chicken, I don't wanna be a duck" dance the next time I flap my elbows with the kids.

The reason: I just rose at 3:30 a.m.—after spending my birthday night in a Craig motel—to witness the mating dance of the greater sage grouse. And you can bet that any gyration tips I glean will make their way to the dance floor.

The trip was put together by Conservation Colorado, which organizes as many as 20 of the outings every year. This one is a special lek tour for members of the outdoor industry; they hope to educate the public and politicians that grouse habitat kicks in $1 billion annually, on federal lands alone, from outdoor recreation.

The term lek is Norwegian for "dance hall." And that's exactly what it is: a place the birds return to every spring for three to five weeks to puff up their chests, shake their tail feathers and woo mates. The one we're heading to is the largest in Colorado.

Not sure what we were getting into, the night before my buddies Johnny, Pete and I YouTubed the mating dance over enchiladas. Johnny then tried to explain in Spanish to our waitress what we'd be watching the next morning. "Baila de amor!" he said, sticking his head out and flexing his chest. To which, not catching the grouse gist, she simply replied, "Otro margarita?"

As proud as peacocks, we told the motel clerk at the Elk Run Inn that we were bird watchers and then settled in for our early morning departure. As if matching our personas with our quarters, Pete's room had a sheep motif; mine a cowboy theme; and Johnny's Jurassic Park ornamentation, complete with Stegosaurus wallpaper and a toothy, T-Rex bedspread.

Catching z's in such a zoo setting is a good precursor to the Mutual of Omaha's Wild Kingdom we soon witness. With stars still shimmering above the City Market parking lot, we pile into several vans and drive north, passing herds of deer, elk and antelope. But since we're here for birds, they don't evoke many oohs and aahs. Next to me is John, a hobby ornithologist freshly off a prairie chicken outing the week before. Today will bring his total to 498 bird species sighted.

"Birding's a big deal," he explains. "People come from all over the world to see this sort of thing. Birders like to notch different species off their list."

Conservation Colorado is hoping to keep the sage grouse off a more important list: The federal government's Endangered Species Act. While Colorado sage grouse numbers rebounded 30 percent this year over last, across the West their population has declined by half over the past century.

In 2010, U.S. Fish and Wildlife deemed them worthy of protection under the Endangered Species Act. But groups like Conservation Colorado and the Western Governors Association, which represents the governors of 19 sage grouse states, feel voluntary efforts will be more effective. Hence, my bleary-eyed ride into the boonies of northwest Colorado, home of two-thirds of the state's sage grouse population.

"Everyone at the table wants to avoid the listing," explains Conservation Colorado wilderness advocate Scott Braden from the front seat, interrupting the stereo's oddly fitting Pink Floyd song for this ungodly hour. "We want what's best for the bird."

On this trip they'll also create a video highlighting the value of sage grouse habitat for the outdoor recreation industry, all in an effort to encourage state and federal officials to protect sagebrush lands. A typical issue of concern, Braden adds, is a new TransWest Express transmission line that would move electricity from a Wyoming wind-power installation to Las Vegas. "It would devastate sage grouse habitat," says Braden.

A half hour later, we turn off said highway west onto a gravel road, then another and another, before stopping at a bumpy two-track. Headlamps pointed to the ground, from here we quietly walk (no rubbing pant legs) a quarter-mile to a special viewing trailer built by the Department of Parks and Wildlife.

We're now at the biggest lek in Colorado. It's on private land, but Conservation Colorado has worked out a deal with the rancher to allow viewings. Quietly bundling up under blankets in the trailer, which feels oddly like sitting inside a Disney simulation ride, we grab our binos and settle in. When we're all set, Braden unlatches two wide metal windows and pivots them open.

Outside it's still pitch black, but the noise hits us like the Road Runner whacking Wile E Coyote over the head. It sounds like a field of popcorn popping, interspersed with high-pitched coos and clucks. It's weirder, even, than the Dark Side of the Moon CD we listened to on the way in.

While we can't see them yet, we know they're there. Soon it lightens and we catch our first glimpse, tiny dots maybe 30 yards away. Then more appear until the whole field is littered with them. And then the show begins.

They strut their stuff, puffing up white fluffy chests, fanning out spiky tail feathers and hopping around like they're on pogo sticks. The field is oozing testosterone and you can tell they're feeling studly. "You lookin' at me?" I imagine them saying in grouse Guido. "How you doing?" It's like the Charles Atlas pectoral flex on the beach, only there are hundreds of them

In all, the organizers count 161 birds today: 123 males and 38 females.

"It sounds like a ski town," whispers Johnny from the bench next to me. "The Old Town Pub on a Saturday night."

Only the birds' odds, while not stellar, are better than those of the typical ski town barfly. Only 25-30 percent of the males will get the job done at any given rendezvous. And us Peeping Toms are hard pressed to see any action; woe of woes, copulation takes only three or four seconds, after which the females promptly leave. Within three weeks they'll lay six to 12 eggs. If grouse smoked cigarettes, this is when the successful males would light up. Cartoonist Gary Larson would have a field day with this species.

In two hours of courtship, we see conga lines, the two-step, line dancing and even a mosh pit when males scurry after other suitors. They flex, swagger, chase and lure, using every trick in the book besides deodorant to consummate a tryst.

At 7:20 a.m., a falcon sends a gaggle flurrying away. Others soon follow suit, leaving only a few wallflowers remaining like late night dancers at a bar. Like the last ones picked for a dodge ball team, a few continue to puff up and look cool before realizing there are no more lasses around to impress.

Soon, we pile out of the trailer into the early morning sunshine. We'd been sitting in the cold for over two hours and welcome its warmth. Shaking the kinks out of my legs and arms, I stick out my chest and do a little jig. Even without their plumage, I can commiserate with their plight.

12 Things To Know About King Solomon Falls

If you haven't visited this iconic waterfall plunge epitomizing Steamboat in the summertime, put it on your huck list and heed the following. If you have been there, you'll still appreciate these finer nuances of one of town's best (until now) kept secrets.

Location, location, location. Despite borrowing its name from King Solomon Creek farther upstream, the main and most user-friendly falls are actually on the Middle Fork of the Little Snake River, which eventually flows by Three Forks Ranch downstream (where the South, Middle and North forks meet). It's nice to know what water is going up your nose.

Ode to the odometer. The dirt road leading to the falls is hard to find. It's a turn-off on the right exactly 10 miles after RCR 129 turns to dirt and you take the left fork just past Columbine Cabins. Once you reach the turn-off, it's about a half mile of moderate 4-wheel-drive road to the parking lot at the trailhead (you can also walk this part). Bonus: the dust on your rear window lets your kids spell their names!

Squash the sandals. The very beginning of the hike involves a steep, loose dirt descent down to the valley floor. Sandals just don't offer enough traction and will send you skidding. Bring an old pair of tennies or full-on river shoes. Hint: don't be afraid to grab bush limbs on the way down.

Compass, schmompass. The trail leading from the parking area is easy to find. But stay to the left at the tiny creek at the bottom of the first steep pitch, which leads to the main trail along the river; the right fork leads up to no-man's land.

Relish the guardrails. Don't worry about burning your coveted Man Card points: grab onto the ropes on the traverses. They're there for a reason. You'll be more humbled (and scraped) sliding down the hill than you will from holding on.

Forsake the foot rungs. Though well-intentioned, a new wooden rope ladder addition to the lone rock scramble descent tends to squish your fingers. It's easier to stay to the well-positioned rock ledges to your right as you descend (our gaggle of 12-year-old girls managed it just fine).

Not taught. Also well intentioned, a new hand line strung above the final log crossing helps escort balancers across the river to the falls. But don't rely on it; it has a fair amount of slack. Yank too hard on it you could end up in the drink.

Pack your pole. And some grasshopper flies. There's a reason Three Forks Ranch just downstream offers some of the best fly-fishing in the country. Cast a hopper along the far cliff to the right as you're looking at the falls and watch the magic happen. Just time your casts between people jumping so you don't snag someone's suit.

One for the money, two for the show really works. The huck is about a 20-footer, but your eyes, of course, are five to six feet above that. On the bright side, you're plunging into perfectly aerated water from the falls, which breaks up the surface tension if not your own. Hint: avoid the dreaded arm slap by bringing them into your chest upon landing.

You're not in Acapulco. Save your vertebrae—and Search and Rescue call—by sticking to the lower jump to looker's left. Plenty of people have gotten seriously hurt by venturing elsewhere, especially to another falls farther upstream. You're a long way from help and Facebook posts from the hospital are out of style.

Sundial science. At 4 p.m at the end of July, the ledge you jump off is still in the sun—but just barely—while everything else is in the shade. And the water is goosebump cold. Plan your warm-bloodedness accordingly.

Follow the same route back. On our last mission, a threesome left 45 minutes before us, but opted to bushwhack past the final steep climb. We each got back to our cars at the same time, much to the kids' delight. Lesson: the steep section is easier on the way up than the way down.

A · I · R
(All Interest/Random)

All Roads Lead to Beer League

Well, it's over. Another winter beer league hockey season has come and gone. And with it, the hopes and aspirations of every team but the one whose name will get enshrined on the coveted Barn Cup trophy and retain bragging rights for the year.

While Steamboat has countless other sports to relive your glory years (if you ever had any), beer league skates away with them all. Entering my 20th year in a league that's getting younger and faster as I get older and slower, with a shot that's off target and fluttering, I can't help but reflect on a few things that make it so special.

• It's the great economic equalizer. You get a range of professions on every team—a veritable cross section of the local workforce. Doctors face off against construction workers, Realtors tussle with lawyers and cooks sit next to CEOs on the bench.

• Free checkups. This year's Team Into the West had three doctors on its roster—Wilkinson, Sisk and Sauerbrey—making it a good team to get hurt against, especially when Dr. Borgerding is reffing. You also can ask about any tweaks you amassed since last time, or that weird bump on your neck.

• It's conducive to post-game suds. Because you have to put on pads, no other sport gives you a half-hour of nearly naked towel talk where you can rehash plays, give teammates grief and even conduct business in the locker room. And each team has its own protocol for who's buying, from roving coolers to an edict requiring bringing beers if you miss a game.

• It has that tough-guy stigma. It's not the thuggish sport you see on TV—"I went to a boxing match and a hockey game broke out"—especially at the town, no-check level. Sure, you might get the occasional poke in the eye with a sharp stick, but pads cushion your falls. And unlike soccer, hoops and softball, the ice glide absorbs the pounding, which is why people play it long after they've hung up their cleats in other sports.

• Built-in heckling sessions—not with your opponents but with your teammates in the locker room. The missed shots, pending engagements, weekend tales, kid travails and sports scores are fair game, as is the subterfuge of sewing your goalie's jersey armpits together so he can better stop slap shots.

• There's parity. Three leagues—A, B and C—invite players of all abilities. Never-evers get the same thrill out of a game as A-leaguers.

• The politics are lax. The A league used to be organized by Pete "The Commissioner" Van de Carr, who, with a fake knee and new Kareem Abdul Jabbar glasses, took no shame in organizing it simply so he could still play, which, much to other team's delight, landed him the goalie spot on our team, the Mad Dogs.

• You get to travel. The six A-league teams play 18 games, including two freezing trips to Craig and several more to the icebox of Oak Creek that culminate with camaraderie in the car and all-you-can-eat Kum & Go hotdogs on the way home.

• Things get heated. Sure, refs have to mop testosterone off the ice sometimes and send grown-ups to the principal's office or the penalty box. But that's what happens when you're flying around with razor blades on your feet and clubs in your hand, and that's what makes it that much more like reliving your childhood. And things always settle down off the ice.

• The players are devoted. Why else would a group called No Bozos put down their Geritol to get up at 5:30 a.m. every Friday to get juked by high schoolers? Why else would otherwise sane adults stay up for 10:15 p.m. Sunday start times? (The key: Don't put your sweatpants on at home.) And why else would Friday noon drop-in sessions fill up on a powder day?

• The memories. You'll either cherish or hide them for life. Like the time I eddied-out kayaking and hiked through the bushes to register, dripping wet with my spray skirt still on, on the last day to sign up for summer league. Or the time I stepped onto the ice with my skate guards on, landing me on my head.

• Scoring feels sweet. Not that I know what it feels like, but especially when it's up on the top shelf where mama keeps the biscuits. So do assists.

• Stinky gear. Even antimicrobial Smartwool base layers don't stand a chance warding off the smell. It's a status symbol of how much you skate.

• The Holy Grail. Every year, it boils down to the quest for the cup: the A league Barn Cup and more Stanley-like B Cup, which is often accessorized with a bra. For the team hoisting it every year, it's the league's crown jewel, your excuse for bailing out on the family. You even get to drink out of it (with plenty of doctors on hand to give you penicillin afterward).

Andre Agassi on Snowboarding

Mountain towns might not be Hollywood (sorry, Aspen), but occasionally, especially in the media biz, you do get to brush elbows with celebrities. I had dinner with Sting once in Telluride—and watched him promptly eject a The Police CD; cooked Lyle Lovett a cheeseburger (yes, he asked for it); gave James Brown a soul brother handshake when he visited his namesake James Brown Soul Center of the Universe Bridge (high-schoolers stuffed the ballot box); and rode the lift with musician Jewel. I once even acted as a ski guide for former Detroit Red Wings captain Dennis Hextall ("You're going to pay for this against the boards tonight," he said when I led him on a post-holing boot hike).

A more intimate encounter came at the World Cup in Beaver Creek, interviewing tennis great Andre Agassi on his newest pursuit off the courts: snowboarding. Dragging his knuckles for less than a year, he took it up after blowing a two-handed kiss to his 20-year professional tennis career, between running his Andre Agassi Charitable Foundation and promoting his book, Open, detailing his use of crystal meth and wearing a wig. Behold snippets from our conversation:

Me: When did you pick up snowboarding?
Agassi: In 2005 I watched my son go out, ride a lift and then disappear for about 45 minutes. I said to myself, 'Hey, I'm missing out on some good times…I'd better learn this.' So I started the next year, and so far I've been out maybe 20-30 times. My father was pretty strict on where he saw me going professionally; I wasn't even allowed to even go off a diving board as a kid. I stayed away from anything that might make my career shorter.

Me: Any similarities between snowboarding and tennis?
Agassi: What I do is hard to consider snowboarding. But it's all problem solving. And you're out there doing it by yourself, so you get to know yourself very intimately.

Me: Any biffs your first few times out?
Agassi: I sure did. I hurt my left wrist my first couple of days and thought I was in for terrible pain on the rest of my falls but it actually got much better. But I'd never been on skis and don't understand the sensation of speed with the body or angles of the mountain, so there were a lot of obstacles to get over. I was proud of myself for pushing through it.

Me: You've won four Grand Slams and are comfortable on any tennis surface. What's your favorite snowboarding surface?
Agassi: Like tennis, some surfaces are certainly different than others. In general, I like anything where if I fall it hurts less. I'll take spring conditions or powder. Then I can start pushing the speed and start pushing myself. But when a fall means pain I get a little tentative.

Me: You're known for a whopping two-handed backhand. So on a snowboard…backside or frontside?
Agassi: I don't have a tremendous about of flexibility. My weakness is getting up after I fall to my heel. I sort of flip over and drop the board down. But I always prefer coming into a heel turn than a toe turn.

Me: Think your heel side will ever rival your backhand?
Agassi: I hope so. My backhand was what got me where I went. To be in the top of any field you have to have something that you count on in a ridiculous way, and you could wake me up in the middle of the night and I'd still go out there and not miss a backhand. But I still miss heel sides.

Me: Who's the Federer of snowboarding…Shawn White?
Agassi: I love that guy. I did a charitable commercial with him for American Express. I don't know if I love his snowboarding more or his hair. I'm envious of both. But what a sweet spirit he is. I don't know him well enough to say if he's the Federer of the sport, but he's amazing.

Me: His hair's kind of like the Agassi of old…
Agassi: Oh, that's generous. You could put his hair in a ponytail and hang

from it. His is quite a bit longer than mine ever was.

Me: You can put backspin on a ball. Tried one on a board yet?
Agassi: Not yet. I prefer anything where I'm not committing myself to having to look down the mountain. I choose old-time tennis…hit the ball very, very flat.

Me: How would you have done in one of these gravity sports?
Agassi: Probably not too well; it's pretty foreign—especially the risk part. You have to have to be born with a special skill set and then nurture it. In tennis I was fortunate with a certain level of eye-hand coordination that was honed early. The part I can identify with is pushing yourself. I considered myself an athlete until I watched these guys.

Me: How'd you find out you had good eye-hand coordination?
Agassi: A lot of Ws. I could always do a few things on the court that other kids couldn't. I hit the ball harder and reacted quicker. As I played older kids my game adapted. You can't let a ball play you, you have to go out to the ball.

Me: Your sponsor Longines' slogan is "Elegance is an Attitude." That apply to snowsports?
Agassi: Looking good is half the battle. If you can't actually do the tricks, it's nice to at least go up the lift. But it's not about how you look, but how you live. It's a great life being out here on the mountain, and it's a great life making a difference in people's lives.

Me: Think you'll ever blow a double-handed kiss to the crowd from your snowboard?
Agassi: Maybe to an imaginary one…I don't think I'm at a gallery any time soon.

An Après for the Ages

It started with the Stammtish and ended with a tennis shoe. In between? More après action than any sane skier could likely squeeze into a season.

In happened while taking a break from living in mountain town and visiting another one: famed St. Anton in the Austrian Alps.

The pace of the evening fit our ski day's. From the 4,000-vertical-foot face of Mount Stuben to hidden couloirs spiraling down to the valley floor, we followed local out-of-bounds outlaw Johnny Spring around like lemmings, bagging and skiing three peaks, all depositing us into different valleys. We stayed with him every step of the way until day's end, when he left us to our own accord.

That brought us to the Crazy Kangaroo bar and its coveted Stammtish, a table reserved for the St. Anton elite. When the bergfuhrers (guides) and Arlberg instructors found us chatting up their dates, their glare was worse than any we encountered on the day's summits. We were politely escorted elsewhere.

That landed us taking up the sport of kegeln, a type of agro-bowling with softball-sized balls. Walled lanes meant no gutters, which meant no inhibitions about letting them rip. Our drinking speed trumped our balls' speed, leading to another polite escort outside.

Unfortunately for our schnitzel-laden stomachs, things picked straight up from there—as in the luge track leading a thousand feet up to a mountainside bar called the Rodelalm. The snowcats hauling tourists up had stopped for the evening, so we hoofed it, adding to the day's vertical. But we didn't exactly re-hydrate at the summit.

"You want the hot stuff?" asked the barkeep, offering us a homemade shot of battery acid, gasoline and flaming pepper juice—a concoction reserved for idiots and Americans, and American idiots like us.

"Sure," we replied. We had survived the skiing, the Stammtish and shoulder-wrenching bowling. Surely we could survive another shot.

Then came our run in with the Austrian Kayaking Team, watching us from the opposite table. Apparently, we seemed like their type.

"And who is your drinking champion?" the leader strode over and asked.

Four of us stepped back, leaving Rob alone to endure another throat-burning elixir. More shots were then poured all around.

That lubricated us for Roller Luge. When the bar closed, and with the Austrian Kayak Team in hot pursuit, we hopped on one-man sleds called rodels down the icy course back to town. Fueled by the flaming shots, we'd get off, hide in the bushes and then blindside each other with James Bond-style body blocks, knocking each other off our sleds. When we finally rolled bruised and battered across the finish line, the clerks issued schnapps with each returned sled.

Our brush with the Mad Austrians wasn't finished.

"And who is your song champion?" bellowed the leader, shot glass in hand. This time it was John left standing on an Austrian hillside, only not quite to the sound of music.

"This is Heinz," he continued. "He is our song champion."

With that, an inebriated Heinz yodeled an Austrian drinking song an inch away from John's face, spewing spittle the entire time. "Not quite the face shots we got skiing Stuben, was it?" Rob said afterward.

By now it was 2 a.m., well past the last train heading down valley to our lodge. No worries, we'd ski the five miles down. The problem was, before our Stammtish debacle I had swapped a ski with John's wife Kristy to thwart thieves, so all I had was that odd-sized pair. The good news: while my ski boot wouldn't fit into her binding, my tennis shoe would.

So that's how I skied it, a Lange in my ski and a Nike in hers. Pitch dark, across sketchy traverses, over spine-compressing whoop-de-dos, one-legging-it across creeks, and at long last, down a crud-filled slope leading to our lodge. When I finally crawled into bed it was 4 a.m. Johnny was picking us up again in two hours. If I left my ski boot on, I'd be that much ahead of the game for the next day...

Bonding on Belay

The storms hurtle by, missing us by mere miles. Rain streaks come between us and Porcupine Rim to the south. Another burst blows by to the north. Had we been in Moab mountain biking as usual, we'd fear mud, a douching and perhaps a case of squeaky brakes.

Instead, we're atop cliff-lined Parriott Mesa, on an area the size of a football field. Three rappels, a via ferrata traverse and an hour of hillside scrambling separate us from the safety of our car.

"Let's get going, boys," says Tristan, a buddy from my Telluride days. "It's moving in pretty quick."

A way better climber than me, with marquee ascents from Yosemite to Fisher Towers, Tristan's been caught topping out in storms before. It's not a good place to be. So we quit gawking at Castle Valley 1,400 feet as the pebble falls below, shush our couch-potato talk of base jumping, and beeline back to the ledge marking our exit. One by one, we clip in our harnesses and rappel off to escape the storm.

There's something about dangling over a void—the type of cliff you'd see in a Road Runner cartoon—connected only to a rope, a couple of anchors and belay device that makes you realize how good you have it in life. The precarious umbilical cord makes you appreciate all the other ties to your existence—your friends, family and home.

The first rappel takes us down through a series of ledges. The second one sandwiches us into a pock-holed slot, protected from the impending storm. A short traverse, including a fixed-rope to help us swing across an exposed span, leads us to the third rappel, which whisks us down an exposed crack, the crux of our climb up. From there we clip into the bolted cable of a via ferrata traverse, re-clipping our slings around each bolted anchor, before finally gaining terra firma on the far side.

"I'm feeling better now," says Drake, another friend and former climbing guide now living in Moab. He's finally breathing easier about lugging us luddites up here.

As far as getting together with the guys, hooking up for a desert climb-hike here was far more rewarding than meeting up in Las Vegas. It let us bond and blaspheme while traipsing around slickrock slots instead of those at gambling halls. And it renewed friendships that time and life obligations had long diluted.

It started the day before when, after meeting, high-fiving and crashing at Drake's house, we headed to Arches National Park to scale its highest point, 5,653-foot Elephant Buttress. From the parking area near Owl Rock, the route first involved winding through a maze of Entrada sandstone fins comprising Bull Winkle rock. A couple of slot grovels later, we tied into our first bolted anchor and rappelled off an 85-foot cliff into a tight ravine. It marked the first time I've ever rappelled down something to get up something. From there, we trusted our shoe's friction to smear our way up another series of twisty canyons and sloping slickrock to the summit.

Lunching up top on BLTs from Moab's Love Muffin, we stared east to Parriott, our next day's quest, before eyeing our alternative route down. The key: locating a freestanding, phallic-looking sandstone spire, marking a final slot canyon rappel. Guarding the rappel's two anchors was a narrow puddle that required a full body stem, hands and feet pressed against opposite walls. Once across, we clipped in and rappelled down the final drop, dangling like spiders over the 60-foot overhang.

Parriott upped the ante a hair, without being overly hairball. A guidebook calls it a premiere "adventure hiking route for experienced hikers, climbers and canyoneers," making it perfect for our multi-abilitied posse.

Stashing our harnesses in our packs after the final traverse, we retrace our uptrail across the desert-red scree field, thankful the sprinkle hasn't loosened any rocks from above. When we finally make it back to the car, we pull out leftover burrito-makings and Budweisers and high-five all around before splitting our separate ways to our respective walks of life. We're no longer connected to our ropes, but our ties to each other are as strong as ever.

Embracing Embarrasments

As I look back on my time spent in Steamboat, it's not life's high points that rise to the surface like a trout taking a fly, but rather its lows. Even more unfortunate is the fact that I have enough of these ignominious moments to share. So I bring them forth unabashedly so that you, too, may feel inclined to do the same.

Tarp Topple: This has to be one of my dorkier happenstances ever. And it caught me by complete surprise. It happened over the summer while shaking out a heavy, dust-covered, canvas paint tarp in the yard—one of those crinkly, paint-splotch-encrusted white ones that had spent too much time rolled up in the shed. All was going well until my third arm-raising, whip-like snap when—raising said tarp with arms extended high above my head—I miscalculated and flapped its near edge held by my hands down straight onto the back of my neck. The blow knocked me flat to the ground instantly, where I laid dazed and perplexed wondering what the heck had happened. Flat on my stomach on the grass and partially covered by the tarp, I was incredulous that such a spastic move had actually happened.

Skate Guard Slip: This one was even more painful. On my first day helping coach my daughter's hockey team, I committed the ultimate, fall-on-your-face faux pas: forgetting to take off one of my skate guards before stepping onto the ice. Before I could say Zamboni, both ankles were six feet high in the air and I came crashing down, padless, onto my side, back and oh-so-tender elbows. Hearing birds tweet, I laid there for a moment before a couple of the girls skated over and said, "That's our coach." Then another added, "That's my dad."

Costume Neck: Me and my dumb costume ideas. This one came while walking around downtown on Halloween as the Upside-down Man, head crammed sideways into the crotch of an upside-down pant leg. Overhead, my shoe-topped hands raised toward the sky and old ski gloves served as my shoes below. The kicker: a Styrofoam mannequin head, complete with wig, attached to a turtle-neck shirt dangling upside-down between my legs. While the effect worked—especially when I wobbled back and forth on my glove-covered feet like I was walking on my hands—the pitfall came at night's end when I pried my poor head out of the angled pant leg. The result: a kinked neck that lasted for days.

Paddle Stick: In the springtime, when the Yampa is swollen with runoff, the back of my car is filled with both kayaking and hockey gear. This incident happened when, subbing in for a town-league team, I showed up groggy at the rink for a 6:30 a.m. game. Reaching into the back of my car, I grabbed my bag and stick and sauntered in, a fellow teammate walking beside me across the parking lot. Only once I sat down in the locker room did I realize my gaffe. "Hey, Eugene, looks like you got the wrong sport," said a teammate. In my hand wasn't my trusty Easton hockey stick, but something else long and skinny instead: my kayak paddle, which I had carried from car to dressing room. "Don't worry," he added. "You might do better with it."

Blind Man's Bluff: Visual impairments are nothing to shake a stick at. I found this out the hard way when my wife and I were walking the wrong way against foot traffic across the 8th Street bridge after the Winter Carnival fireworks show (my wife wanted to find our daughter at Howelsen). After she ditched me through the crowd, I stayed behind waiting on the Howelsen side of the footbridge overlooking the skate park. The linchpin to my predicament was the ski pole I had brought along to nurse a sore knee. After waiting a half hour, I got restless—as any husband would—and began fidgeting, whacking the nearby snow bank back and forth with my pole. That's when a man in the throng walking by grabbed my shoulder, spun me around, and pointed me toward the bridge. "The bridge is this way!" enthused Mr. Good Samaritan, thinking I was blind and poling the bank for bearing.

Snowboard Skate: Walk up Blackmere Drive as a snowboarder in the winter and you can't help but think how fun it would be to slash fresh turns down the powdery snowbanks lining each side of the road. So I made it more time efficient by skate skiing up the road with my snowboard strapped to my back. (Note to self: it's more awkward than it sounds; your elbows hit the board every stride.) Up top, I wedged two pieces of Ensolite foam into my snowboard bindings so my skate ski boots would fit, then I shoved off—skis in one hand and poles in the other—making my mark on every side hill. It was all fine and dandy until my anonymity was exposed halfway down. "Is that Eugene?" asked a member of a girls' group out for their daily stroll. "What on earth are you doing?"

Kayak Rescue At Bruce's: I owe this one to my early-season, skate skiing buddy Paul. On fine November afternoon we were skate skiing Bruce's Trail when he biffed on that last, fast downhill turn on the short loop, crashing into a tree and tweaking his knee so bad he couldn't finish skiing out. Fortuitously enough, my car at the trailhead was loaded with kayaks I was planning to review on the Colorado River in Glenwood. So I skated skied out with a friend, grabbed a kayak from the top of the car, hooked it up to a rope, and towed it behind us back to Paul. There, we loaded him up ski patrol sled-style and towed him back to the parking lot.

Embracing Your Steamboat Zen

Blame it on my Boulder upbringing. How else would you explain my jumping at the chance to hop in a giant clam to test the new, space-age float tanks at Neptune Healing and Float Spa downtown?

The company hangs its fedora on float therapy, a treatment dating back to Cleopatra floating in the Dead Sea. The premise: completely deprive your senses—sight, sound, smell and even feel—allowing your body and mind to relax and heal.

They do this via two time machine-looking float pods filled with 900 pounds of magnesium sulfate (epsom salts) and 10 inches of water heated to your exact body temperature, creating the sensation that body and water are one. Quadruple-cleaned after each session with ultraviolet light, ozone and two filters, the sterile solution lets you float free of gravity and other stimuli, much like returning to the womb. This lets your brain waves shift from the active Beta to the slower Theta state associated with meditation. The magnesium sulfate also loosens muscles and relieves tension, depression and anxiety.

Sign me up, said Birkenstock-wearing Boulder Boy, when owner Valerie McCarthy suggested sampling the treatment. I even convinced my overly stimulated 16-year-old daughter to put Siri to sleep and tag along.

First came a quick introduction to the facility. Partner Brian Savoie, who works in the hospital's MRI department so is well familiar with capsules and energy waves, said there are a variety of tanks to choose from, but that they went with the Porsche version, the largest and best available. They got the idea after hopping in a tank in Denver (there are also two—surprise!—facilities in Boulder) and deciding it would be perfect for Steamboat's active residents.

Next, we watched a short video hosted by the animated "Float

Guru." We learned we'd shower before and after the 60-minute float and that we'd likely assume one of three customary positions: the Plank (hands by your side), I Surrender (hands by your head), and Mummy (hands folded across your stomach). And since we'd be enclosed in our own pod in a private room, we might as well go in our birthday suits to further eliminate sensation (like I'd even feel my thong). The video also advised counting 300 breaths to help unleash our inner Zen.

Climbing in, I couldn't help but remember that '80s flick Altered States, starring William Hurt as a Harvard scientist whose experiments with hallucinogens and isolation chambers cause him to regress genetically. I didn't think I could get any more Cro-Magnon than I already was, crawling inside a giant clamshell naked.

With that, I closed the hatch and assumed the position. Meditative music played for the first five minutes as I settled in, then all went dark and quiet. While you can do it with muted lights and your own music, I took their advice and went full commando for full deprivation mode.

McCarthy said it takes some time to get in the groove, and that's what I found. "I have an hour of this?" I thought, as I fidgeted to get comfortable. My mind raced as I first tried the Plank position: "Pick up eggs, mow the lawn, call that guy, fix the garbage disposal, buy a patch kit, email whoshewhatsit." Finding that position to be too tense on my neck, I shifted to I Surrender and instantly all was right with the world. I heard my heart beating and my breathing, my brain waves aligning with each. I tried counting breaths, but only made it to 20 before my mind wandered like a deer prancing through a field of wildflowers.

Despite being from Boulder, and once actually owning an incense burner, I've never been much of a meditator. But with all sensory input eliminated, I was nam-myoho-renge-kyo-ing with the best of them.

Research abounds on the therapy's benefits. Invented in the 1950s by Dr. John Lilly, the brainwave researcher who prompted the movies Altered States and The Day of the Dolphin, they're gaining steam for their ability to decrease pain, anxiety and depression and elevate mood. Athletes worldwide are even embracing them for training. The Dallas Cowboys, Philadelphia Eagles, Seattle Seahawks and New England Patriots all have tanks, letting the likes of Tom Brady heal while contemplating DeflateGate free of gravity. Olympic sprinter Carl Lewis even float tanked to get his brain on the right track before running on one. And their effects are cumulative; by the third float, chronic pain reportedly drops by 90 percent.

I kept waiting for something else to drop, like my butt and feet, but they never did; the 38 percent salt solution kept them from sinking, with only my eyes, nose and mouth above the surface. My ears, plugged to keep the salt out, rested just below, muffling all sound except that coming from my body. The only extraneous sensation was the occasional toe-brush against the pod's wall.

Never touching the optional light button or Intercom, my mind swirled with the water, progressing from the busy fraternity of Beta waves to more thoughtful Theta. That's the only way to explain how quickly the music and lights came back on, signaling the hour was up.

Taking in my tranquil surroundings for a few more minutes, I then opened the rounded hatch, rejoining the over-stimulated world. Showering off the salt, I zombied back to the reception room and waited for my daughter, who embraced it as much as I did, no easy feat for an Instagramming teen.

"Did you twitch?" asked Savoie, as McCarthy clanged giant gongs for the final *pièce de résistance* (she also practices sound healing therapy).

Indeed I did, at one point both my foot and shoulder involuntarily rippling the water. "So did I," gushed my daughter, any embarrassment we might have felt flushing through the filter with the water.

"That's good," said Savoie. "That's what happens when you enter Theta."

Driving home, readjusting to the stimulations of the "big city," I glanced at the river by the library. Tubing the Yampa, I realized, isn't the only way to get in a relaxing float in Steamboat.

End of a Coaching Era

Well, I've done it. I've done gone and reached the end of soccer coaching era in Steamboat.

With the end of the Steamboat Soccer Tournament July 13-15, which drew 120 teams from across the West, my daughter Casey has officially graduated from rec level to competitive. And that means she, and the rest of her teammates, need someone with a little more coaching cred than I have. A few more soccer stripes. Someone whose career spans more than playing for the Boulder High Bagels and Bongs intramural teams.

I knew the day was coming. I coached my daughter Brooke's teams from age 5 to 10 also, before, she, too, moved on to greener coaching pastures. Then I was relegated back to the minors to begin the coaching cycle all over again.

But it was a good run, even if it meant tying more shoelaces than teaching soccer skills. And the kids got better each year, until they could juggle better than I could —thanks to their growth spurts more than any words of wisdom I imparted.

But there are things I will surely miss. Like answering incessant questions about shirt, shorts and sock colors, or coming home from a game with a pocketful of earrings, scrunchies and hair clips, begrudgingly taken off by the girls in front of the ref at midfield.

No more array of lost water bottles to clutter our mudroom cubbies. No more losing program-issued soccer balls, sheepishly returning an empty net bag at season's end.

No more admonishing someone to stop blowing dandelions or counting lady bug spots in the middle of a game. No more asking for team name ideas only to see 15 hands shoot in the air with different suggestions. And no more having to settle for the less-than-intimidating Pink Petunias only to face the Annihilating Death Ninjas in game one.

No more catching grief for showing up with a rubber band still around my pants leg from biking. No more balls disappearing down a flooding Spring Creek, prompting a safety talk from a fireman warning not to retrieve them. No more bears disrupting practice. No more reprimanding my daughter and her friends when they showed up late the first time they walked from school to practice, unbeknownst to me stopping in the school nurse's office to treat a scraped knee.

No more studying the coach's manual and improvising such skills-building games as Red Light/Green Light, Pac Man, Red Rover, Simon Says, Bombs Away, and the kids' favorite Cream the Coaches. No more four count burpies, evoking actual burps, during warm-ups.

No more team cannonballs into the D-hole after a game. No more having only one practice on grass before the Grand Junction tournament, the rest coming on scoria-filled parking lots (coach's note: bring more Band-aides). No more admitting to Alzheimer's by trying in vain to remember who substituted for whom when in a game (coach's hint: use interchangeable wrist bands with positions written on them).

No more cringing at your team's goal kicks, knowing the other team will likely pounce on it and score because it will only dribble a few yards. No more getting trounced at tournaments, getting one shot off in three games, only to see our kids still have the time of their lives. No more playing sharks and minnows in overly chlorinated hotel swimming pools, while "resting up" for the next morning's game. No more watching the girls come up with their own cheer and dance for other team, or basking in a lone tournament victory.

No more group camping in Grand Junction, skateboarding with lacrosse sticks behind bikes, organizing the world's biggest water fights, carbo-loading with s'mores, and sneaking off to mountain bike Fruita or the Lunch Loops.

Sure, I'll still do some of these things in my continued role as a parent instead of a coach. But I'll cheer on neutrally for "Steamboat" from the sidelines instead of calling out instructions.

As far as playing out-of-town teams, I hope my record doesn't speak for itself; we got crushed by those that play year-round. But while my coaching techniques might not follow the system that leads players to a pro career, I like to think they instilled a love for the game, helped them work as a team and, above all, helped them have fun.

In a 10-year coaching run, I learned more from them than they did ever from me, and I look forward to seeing them progress even further as the next coaches take the reins. And girls, call me anytime if you're still missing a scrunchie.

Freedom Points

How do you get your own recreation in once you have kids in a mountain town? It boils down to freedom points: an unofficial tally of how much you've watched the kids compared to how much your spouse has.

The math is simple: You earn them by riding herd on your brood, and you spend them by recreating. It follows an unspoken law of supply and demand: If they're there, you can use them; if the supply's run dry, so have your chances of Me-time.

The rules are simple. Like exercising a stock option, they have a finite redemption period, usually no more than a week or two. Try to cash in on that time spent babysitting three months ago and you'll be met with a glare. They're like sick days at work. Use them or lose them. They don't carry over, and they don't grow interest. So spend them quickly. That hour you watched the kids last night? Turn it into a jog the next day.

Another trick of the now-laden-with-toddler trade: Spend them wisely. Don't waste them on something you could've normally done anyway; that's like spending birthday money on your mortgage. If you somehow earned a four-hour window, don't burn them on the same short bike ride you always do. Do something bigger. And don't waste them on something you could have done anyway—like that quick jog on the bike path. Freedom points earned should equal freedom points well spent. It's an art form, with the experts going to creative extremes to spend their ounces of freedom.

They also teach you to be more efficient. You'll stop the meter from running as soon as possible. No more lingering at the Town Challenge bike race party after your ride; instead, you'll return home at a reasonable, Ward Cleaver hour. You'll squeeze in paddling sessions between Pampers and mountain bike rides between milk bottles. You'll also go solo more, whenever your window allows, and with people who don't waste your valuable time. No more waiting for someone's misplaced shuttle keys or perpetual flat tire. Match every tick of the clock with a schuss of the ski or crank of the wheel.

And you'll master your short game. Out-of-town, farther-from-family adventures might suffer, but you'll pursue micro adventures closer to home, discovering a host of activities overlooked until parenthood.

The best-case scenario is when you can squeeze something in without burning points, like sneaking out at lunch for a ride when you would've been away from family anyway. Better yet is earning points while you're recreating, like I thought I did when it was my time to watch her but instead I pawned her off on a babysitter and went biking. But it was a tough sell to the jury back home.

A White Elephant Gun Case

If grandma-who-got-run-over-by-a-reindeer got what I got for Christmas, that reindeer would have ended up a trophy above her mantle.

Forget the in-laws, last minute shopping and stress of frothing your meringue to a pointed whip. The real test to the holidays is surviving the White Elephant gift exchange.

While music teacher Donald Gardner championed two front teeth in his holiday classic, you usually walk home with a lot weirder wares than that. For us this season it was a gun case that we walked—or rather, trailered—away with after one of the wackier White Elephant weeks we've ever endured.

For those not familiar with this ritual that has trumpeted its way into holiday parties nationwide, here's some beta. The term purportedly comes from sacred white elephants kept by Southeast Asian monarchs as a sign of power. Whenever someone received one as a gift, it was both blessing and curse—a sign of the monarch's favor, but expensive to maintain.

Churches held "white elephant sales" in the early 19th Century, with businessman Ezra Cornell brainstorming the gift-exchange concept in 1828. The time-honored gist: each participant supplies a gift and then draws a number determining who picks when. After the first person opens a gift, the next person can either steal it or choose a different one. If yours gets stolen, you can steal another or go back to the wrapped pile (never mind that it encourages your kids to steal).

This year we certainly did our part in keeping the tradition alive—even though we ended up with a case for things that can kill. We had two of the junk-accumulating affairs back-to-back, barely leaving us time to shelf the first fruits (or fruitcake) before carting home more clutter.

The first was at a friend's Christmas Eve party, involving store-bought presents with a monetary cap. While this ensures a level playing field, it also ensures a few items that belong in the Milner Mall. After drawing straws to see which adult had to don the Santa suit and deliver the gifts, my daughters stole both presents and the show. After a 15-year-old boy named Cash ended up with an M&M dispenser, Casey, 10, eyed it wistfully but didn't want to hurt his feelings by stealing it. After some reassuring, she mustered up the courage and repossessed it, leaving Cash to begin anew.

Casey's teenage sister Brooke had no such qualms, promptly stealing Casey's hard-won pride and joy to a chorus of boos. Justice prevailed when a downtrodden Casey opened another present to find a One Direction calendar, featuring 12 floppy-haired months of Brooke's favorite band. "Oh yeah, Bu-yeah!" she flaunted in Brooke's direction, vindicating her sibling's M&M malfeasance. As if this wasn't St. Nick magic enough, negating all the Seven Deadly Sins on display that evening, the spirit of Christmas was further renewed later that evening when Brooke, on her own accord, appeared in our wrapping room and proceeded to wrap the M&M dispenser to give back to a heartbroken Casey.

The next night had even more drama, perhaps because of its caveat requiring the gift to come from your home. Choosing one of the most immaculately wrapped presents of the lot, Casey opened hers to find inside a framed, smiling photo of the giver, teenage Koby, straight from his family's photo wall. Her rejection was as palpable as the eggnog.

After no one else stole it (surprise), feeling pity I sacrificed my own chance at stardom by stealing Koby's beaming picture, leaving Casey free to choose the last gift from the pile, an innocuous-looking, ribbon-tied bag. Inside was a card reading "Door #1!" With that, the host and a sturdy friend disappeared down a hallway and returned minutes later rolling in— you guessed it—a full-sized, floor-to-ceiling, glass-windowed wooden gun case. While perfect, perhaps, for the Nerf gun Casey opened that morning, it wasn't perfect for our freshly de-cluttered household. It dwarfed our Subaru outside and took two grown men to carry. Casey had added to her M&M bounty with the night's biggest, if not best, prize.

I, meanwhile, left with Koby's pearly whites, Brooke a brownie-making pan, and my wife a fax machine even the local thrift store shunned. (As we drove home with bounty in hand, Casey asked from the back, "What's a facts machine, anyways? A machine you ask, 'What's the color of a lemon?' and it tells you, 'yellow?'")

More importantly, this gift of a game from the monarchs left us with a new appreciation for a tradition that—if you can overlook the clutter it creates and moral compass it steers astray—actually keeps the spirit of Christmas alive. Even if your present facilitates hunting reindeer.

Humbled By The Hockey Clock

It's part of living here as a parent...volunteering to help your kid's sport. No matter that it also counts against your work deposit, negating any altruism. If your kid's on a team, it's your God-given, Steamboat-living duty to help out.

My role this year just happened to be a tad more complicated than most: it involved the dreaded Time Clock at Howelsen Ice Arena.

In soccer, you might man the concession stand, pump up a ball or sub in as a line judge ("That way, I mean that way!" you point the flag). But the dreaded Time Clock? No one steps up for that one. Come tournament time, it's the last spot filled on the spread sheet, the Hades of helping, the Voldemort of volunteerdom.

The reason I even took the spot is I had already failed at the easier task of announcing, manning the mic and music. While I played We Will Rock You, the Rocky theme and girlie hip-hop well enough, I was a tad zealous with the actual announcing, play calling like you hear on the radio: "Pataznick over to Johnson, Johnson back to Pataznick, Oh! What a save!" Only it wasn't the radio; you're not supposed to do that live, on-site. My phone buzzed with texts from the volunteer manager in the stands: "No announcing, no announcing!"

So I gave in and tried my hand at the Time Clock, even taking the little training course from Metzy beforehand. After all, if he could figure it out, I certainly could. Fat chance. It all looked so simple then, watching his pudgy little fingers push various buttons here and there and then the corresponding numbers all show up perfectly on the scoreboard for all to see.

But it's a whole new ballgame when you're on your own in front of refs, coaches and, worse, hockey parents.

To start with, it's always in winter, in the cold end of the rink, with your time somehow always starting at 6 a.m., when even roosters' gullets are frozen shut. So you bundle up and position yourself between two archaic space heaters just a breath carry's away from the world's slowest-closing door.

Once you settle in, and rub your hands together a few times, the other team's managers and coaches filter in, sharing cordialities (and forgetting to shut the door). But all such niceties end there if you so much as miss a paltry second on the Time Clock.

Begrudgingly, you cowboy up for the task, wary of the electronic box all innocent-looking in front of you. A simple look at it begins the jitters; it has more buttons than the NORAD defense system.

It's an All Sport 4000 Series Control Console by Daktronics, with buttons for each team, so multiply the aggregate finger-pushing total by two. There are buttons for Player Penalty, Disable Player Penalty, Enable Player Penalty, Score +1, Period +1, Clear/No, Enter/Yes, Set Main Clock, Start/Stop, Horn, Main Menu, Shots on Goal and more, as well as cursor and scroll arrows to navigate the navigation screen.

First you have to program in the rules of engagement: a three-minute warm-up, run time; first two periods 14 minutes run time, meaning the clock keeps going unless there's an injury or the ref stops play because you're a doofus; third period 12 minute stop time, unless one team has a four-point lead in which case the Mercy Rule kicks in and it reverts to run time. And that all changes depending whether it's league or tournament play. Really, guys?

Thrown to the wolves, you set it at five minutes for warm-up time... oops...should be three, so re-set the manual clock. Thank God it's only 14-year-old girls playing—who can get that worked up over a missing practice second here or there? Nothing against the girls and their fine abilities, it's just a hair less serious than, say, the high school state championships. I probably should have started on a game for six-year-olds.

Warm-up time inputted, it's time to move onto the actual periods. Let's see, is it 14 stop, 14 stop and 12 run; or 12 stop, 12 stop and 14 run? Or 14, 14 and 14 run? Or should I just run? And all bets are off, heaven forbid, if there's a penalty to input, let alone two at the same time. Enable Player Penalty, Enter/ Yes, Enter Jersey Number, Enter/Yes, Enter/Yes. (You have to hit that Enter button twice the last time.) Then hopefully 2:00 pops up on the scoreboard before the ref drops the puck, forcing you to hit the Start/Time button again. So you hedge your bet by scribbling down the clock time on a piece of paper just in case, so you know when to let the poor bugger back out into society.

You also have to know how to get rid of a penalty if the other team scores, beginning a whole new era of button-pushing and mistake-canceling (today, I wish I had a "Jensen" button to push, the big bruiser).

Eventually, if you're lucky, you might get it right. And you get a warm fuzzy when you see the two minutes pop up on the scoreboard just like they're supposed to and actually start ticking off in perfect unison with the time clock on the All Sport 4000 Series Control Console by Daktronics. It's not like you found the cure for cancer or anything, but it's a feeling of accomplishment all the same.

At one point (sorry, visiting Eagle Valley) I neglected to start the clock correctly, letting the game accrue 30 extra seconds. But in the grand equaling- out-of-things, I cheated ahead a few seconds during the next few puck-drops until all was more or less even-Steven.

It's the stop time that's hard; more so than even the players, you have to pay attention to every whistle. During run time, you can kick back and relax, entering an occasional score or penalty here and there between sips of coffee. Stop time makes you regret that margarita the night before; it takes your full mental faculties. No day-dreaming, no spacing out, just eye on the game and finger on the button at all times.

Eventually, you'll make it through the first period with only a few scoldings. Then you'll push the second and third period buttons until, miracles of miracles, the buzzer sounds the end of the game with the score correct and everything. You'll let out a sigh of relief, leaving it just like you found it for the next poor soul working off their deposit hours. So, too, will the unfortunate, parental sap next to you running the Sport-Ngin Point Streak system, who kept track of jersey number changes, player scratches, goals, assists and shots for the ever-important 14-year-old girls' stat sheet.

The good news, and volunteer validation, for me came that night when watching a Denver University/St. Cloud game on TV. At one point the announcers said the penalty clock was broken, which is why it didn't show on the scoreboard. Yeah, right...it was probably some poor schmuck of a parent just like me.

If I Had a Million Dollars

In the whirlwind, hustle-bustle social scene of the holiday season, which now sees more people stream into town than ever, you never know who you might brush elbows with in the lift line, après lounge or, in my case, someone's living room.

While rumors circled of the Duck Dynasty flock and wild-haired Sam Bush ringing in E3 Chophouse's gala opening downtown, not being in that steakhouse social circle left me to my own devices diving into the new year, one that I wouldn't trade for a million dollars.

Turns out, Jim Creeggan of the Barenaked Ladies was in town with his family for the holidays, staying at the well-appointed second home of his in-laws. He had a grand old time in this hamlet of ours, enjoying copious snow, sunshine and even an invitation to play in the annual A-B-C hockey tournament with his then 9-year-old son, Finn (they're Canucks, after all—they'll often rustle up games on tour, giving concert tickets to entice local goalies to play).

And that's what somehow got me and our far-from-polished, mid-life crisis band El Kabong invited to said house, complete with Chesterfields and ottomans, on January 1 for a New Year's party. Sure enough, faster than we could raid the hors d'oeuvre table he soon grabbed a bass and joined us on the makeshift living room stage, where I quickly made the most of the opportunity.

As an aspiring campfire guitarist and not much more, I'd had their marquee, three-chord "If I Had a Million Dollars" song in my repertoire for some time. So we broke it out. Because if any of us actually had a million dollars we'd likely spend it playing that song with a member of the Barenaked Ladies. With the band strumming the monotonous G,C,D progression (it has an E-minor that we ignore), we launched in.

The song first came about as an improvisation composed by band members Steven Page and Ed Robertson while working as counselors at a summer music camp. Robertson played it for the campers, randomly listing things he'd buy with a million dollars, and then fleshed it out some more with Page. It's since become as much of a Canadian icon as Wayne Gretzky and Tim Hortons.

So the same day I got a mullet (yes, that's true, but a different story) I found myself playing If I Had a Million Dollars with Creeggan as my doo-whopping back-up (with additional harmony courtesy of party-goer Sam Pearson). No sooner than the first lyric came out, he laughed and joined in flawlessly, complete with an impromptu chorus about the party's bacon-wrapped hors d'oeuvres, which we could eat in the tree fort in the yard.

In my 15, fleeting minutes of fame, I thought of a few other ways to spend the money in town, most of which didn't make it through the microphone. While it certainly wouldn't go as far as it did when the Barenaked Ladies first recorded the song in 1992, if I had a million dollars to spend in Steamboat, I'd (please voice-over in proper timing and high-pitched tune): donate it to the Sports Club; build a new road to Emerald Park; build a boat ramp to the Yampa; invest it in our local trails; buy me a Moots (or an Eriksen); get a snowcat for Buff Pass; hire someone to shovel our berms; find a home for our police station; and fish private water all season long.

The list could go on and on, but I didn't want to bore him with the nuances of our town. So we wrapped it up with the monkey ("haven't you always wanted a monkeeey?") and the sappy bit about love.

I doubt his standing-in topped the Champagne powder he skied, the hockey tournament he played in or the town's genuine good-naturedness he found on every corner. He may well even boycott Steamboat for good now thanks to my hack job. But there's also a slim chance that he liked what he saw here in Ski Town USA, if not what he heard. And if that's the case, someday, once his eardrums heal, he might even return, in a nice reliant automobile or a limousine because it costs more.

Labor Day at Flaming Gorge

"This is flaming gorgeous!"

The one-liner comes from my daughter, Casey, as we motor our pontoon boat 13 miles up Utah's Flaming Gorge Reservoir to Carter Creek. Out of the wind rippling the main lake, the side canyon snakes through a Christmas scene of red cliffs flanked by pinyon pine. We shut off our engine a few bends back where the creek plunges in like Santa's beard. To the side, other visitors are cannonballing off a 25-foot cliff into the water.

The canyon's two unofficial campsites are occupied, one under an overhang and another by the cascading creek. No matter. We're here on a day jaunt from our camp at Mustang Ridge, happy to be exploring one of Steamboat's best kept weekend secrets. We unload our sea kayak and paddleboard and paddle and swim away the afternoon, using our boat as a reggae-blaring base camp for beverages and lunch.

We've come here—my family of four, as well as another family of five—on an impromptu Labor Day weekend because, well, after two decades of living in Steamboat, we've never been here to Steamboat's mountain version of Lake Powell. All that changed when Casey's soccer team bowed out of Denver's President's Cup early, leaving Labor Day free for the first time in years. So camping it was.

Which is one of the best things about Flaming Gorge: It's close enough that you can rally on a moment's notice.

While you can drive here via Vernal, the quickest way is to turn right onto Colorado Highway 318 right after Maybell, and stay on it an hour and a half through Brown's Park (note: take your potty break beforehand). This is where Butch Cassidy's Wild Bunch hunkered down, for good reason: it's barren, remote and perfect for outlaws; and they could escape jurisdiction by border-hopping between Wyoming, Utah and Colorado.

Eventually you'll take a left on U.S. Highway 191 and catch your first glimpse of the sparkling lake at Antelope Flats. From there, it's onto your campsite at either Mustang Ridge or Cedar Springs, which stare at each other across a bay. Cedar Ridge is closer to the marina and its quaint floating bar and restaurant, while Mustang has better access to the water.

We were happy with Mustang, especially when we discovered a short hike leading to cliff jumps and a beach called Sunny Cove, where we stashed our paddlecraft to use throughout the weekend. Other campers at Cedar Springs, we'd learn, would even drive over to Sunny Cove for the day.

Arriving in the early afternoon, we called my friend Gary (yes, there's cell service), who has the scene dialed. Most summer weekends he camps wherever he wants along shore with his family in their houseboat and speed boat. "Look across the bay," he said. "That's us in our own private cove." Fifteen minutes later they arrived at our camp to take the kids tubing and cliff jumping.

In the morning, I sea kayaked 20 minutes over to their camp, while the rest of our clan drove. Today was pontoon boat day, a 25-footer that fit us and our toys. While Gary paralleled us up the gorge buzzing the kids around on tubes, we explored the reservoir's hidden bays and coves on our way up to Carter Creek.

Like catching the last chair up Storm Peak, we returned the boat five minutes before its 6 p.m. deadline, before visiting three other Steamboat families camped at a group site at Cedar Springs. They've been coming here every Labor Day for years and it shows. Teens are devouring pot luck fajitas, grown-ups are tossing horse shoes and youngsters are whipping around the campground on bikes.

Back at our own camp, Paul and I head out under the stars for a late night sea kayak and paddleboard by Braille. It's calm and serene, with the dam lights across the bay joining the reflection of the twinkling stars.

The Flaming Gorge Dam, of course, is why we're even camping here. Completed in 1964, it's named for a now-buried canyon discovered by John Wesley Powell on his first descent of the Green River in 1869. Towering 502 feet tall and 1,285 feet long, it backs up water 91 miles into Wyoming, submerging four gorges of the Green.

It's one of six dams in the Colorado River Storage Project, a mid-1900s plan created by the Bureau of Reclamation to store and distribute upper Colorado River Basin water. Any sentimental feelings I might have about its buried canyons are washed away knowing it was a compromise for the Echo Park Dam not getting built 50 miles downstream in Dinosaur National Monument.

The next morning we get a taste of what was lost. After updating our fly collection at Johnny Spillane's fly shop, Trout Creek Flies, in Dutch John, we put our raft in below the dam to float the seven-mile A stretch of the Green. While the reservoir is one of Utah's greatest fisheries, the cold, emerald-green water released from the dam's 131-foot-thick base has transformed 28 miles of the Green into one of the best trout fishing floats in the country.

The night before at Cedar Springs, my friend Todd had given me his hand-tied secret weapon: a cranefly larva nymph, to dangle six feet off a hopper. That I did, double checking my knot to not lose the gift.

Guiding eight of us in a paddle raft while trying to cast didn't leave me with much of a gift for fishing. But it did for Paul, who quickly put Todd's creation to work by landing a 17-inch rainbow. The kids were just as interested in the river's beaches, canyon, rapids and swimming holes as they were our fishing exploits.

All too soon we reached the take-out at Little Hole, which marks the put-in for the B section. There, we begrudgingly packed up and headed home after a weekend as packed as our car, arriving just in time to make the kids' school lunches.

While our freshly skunked dog reminded me how I fared fishing, it didn't get me down. We had rafted, fished, motor-boated, tubed, sea kayaked, paddleboarded, camped, biked and more, all on an impromptu weekend visiting one of Steamboat's unsung jewels.

Just as she did with her flaming-gorgeous comment on the boat, Casey summed it up as I tucked her in: "We should do that every year!"

Play well in your soccer game but lose, sweetheart, and maybe we can.

Learning While Turning

It's December 17, finals day at Mr. Travis Moore's geology class at Aspen High. He takes attendance, and to no surprise all 16 students are present. Even Ferris Bueller wouldn't miss this one.

"Not many students play hooky today," he admits to me in row three after roll call. Then he turns back to his charges: "Who still owes me a permission form? Everyone have a pencil? Don't bring pens—it's too cold."

It's hard to get the students' attention in Room No. 1198 today. Sure, they're taking their end-of-semester final. But they're doing it on the ski slopes.

After Moore explains the procedure, the students grab their skis from haphazard positions against the walls and head outside to the Five Trees chair leading to Highlands' Thunderbowl. It's just a spitwad shot away, and likely the closest lift to a high school in the world. "This is the sweetest way to take a test ever," says snowboarder Vinny Johnson, shuffling to the lift in green-checkered pants, braces and helmet.

That the school's mascot is the Skiers and its race team has pocketed seven state championships shows at the top of the lift when patrols open the thigh-deep bowl for the first time all year. If this is the first part of the test, there's no bell curve—everyone passes equally, with Moore, who once won the Grand Traverse race and starred in the movie Mountain Town, laying S-turns on the far side. By the time they're finished the slope is crisscrossed with tracks as if Moore has proven the Pythagorean Theorem on a chalkboard.

"At first, I was convinced I'd get fired," Moore says as we ride the Exhibition lift. "So we just did it under the radar. I still get crap from other teachers, but mostly they're just jealous."

He now has the administration's full endorsement. In fact, playing hooky next to us is assistant principal Brad Bates, not about to miss the chance to tag along. "From the outside, it might not seem very academic," Bates admits. "But it sinks in more this way."

The students' skis then do their own sinking-in as they schuss to Station No. 1 atop Snyder's Ridge. There, with avalanche bombs echoing off Highlands Bowl, they break into teams of two and pull out the five-page exam. Question No. 1: What is the name of the valley below us? (Answer: Castle Creek.) Question No. 2: What type of glaciation has occurred here? (Answer: Glacial trough.) Station No. 2 is at Five Towers, where a snowboarder grinds a mini-cornice behind Moore. Clouds roll in and obscure Pyramid Peak, but not enough to obscure the answers. What's the semi-circular basin called near the top of Sievers Ridge? What mineral is responsible for the rocks' color?

Then it's off to the final station atop Golden Horn, where a couple of students crawl inside a patrol shed to pen their answers out of the wind. Then, one by one they turn in their exams.

"Can we go now?" asks one, getting ready to ski away, semester complete.

"Hold on!" yells Moore, collecting the tests. "Make sure to turn in your books and rock projects."

Skiing geology finals aren't the only experiential offering at Aspen High. In a program called the Al Johnson Challenge (named after the valley's famous skiing postman), Bates helps students build 12 pairs of skis in wood shop, complete with custom graphics, and then leads them on a hut trip to test the fruits of their labor. "Only one pair fell apart," says Bates. "But the kid was doing front flips on them."

Maddy's Misfortune

Some wedding table conversations are better than others. Still, none of us at Table 9 were prepared for the doozy related by John "Maddy" Madigan, a not-too-backcountry-savvy friend from Seattle.

The story began simply enough, barely giving us pause from our plates. But then our attention was grabbed and dragged along like snowflakes in an avalanche. Before long, we were sitting enthralled, ignoring the toasts and speeches around us.

It all started on Presidents' Day when Maddy and his friend, Greg, decided to take a day trip and ski from Mount Bachelor's Edison Snowpark to a warming hut six miles away. "What probably started it all," said Maddy, skewering a piece of salmon, was a 5-liter box of Mountain Chablis."

The events that followed could likely be traced to their decision to chug from the box whenever they saw a blue diamond trail marker. "It was sort of like playing Bob on the Bob Newhart Show," he said. "Only instead of drinking when you hear 'Bob,' we did it when we saw trail markers."

On a well-marked trail, it didn't take long for the Chablis to go to their heads, which led to another innovative way to kill time: taking turns making up stories, which always ended the same way—one guy would get hurt while the other wound up in a hot tub with the girls. Skiing, chatting and drinking with nary a care, time passed as quickly as the wine and they soon found themselves at the open-walled hut warming themselves around a cast iron woodstove. After venturing outside to purge himself of Chablis, Maddy returned and noticed that his friend was warming his hindquarters by the stove.

"It looked warm and toasty," said Maddy, "so I dropped my pants also and started moving my butt back and forth over the stove. But then I lost my footing and fell cheek-first on the thing."

Picture the almost-audible ass hiss. And it gets worse. Since the stove was low and at an angle, and he didn't want to put his hands on it to push off, Maddy had to rock himself back and forth to finally stand back up, exasperating the situation. He then waddled outside and planted his derriere in the snow to an eruption of steam. When he returned, the two laughed at his misfortune in a drunken stupor. "But it hurt like hell," he said.

Wine gone and butt burnt, reality set in and it was time to ski back to the car. By now, however, it had started getting dark and five inches of fresh snow had covered the trail. With seared hindquarters and Chablis-filled legs, Maddy didn't do so well and fell down constantly. Then the sun went down, and in the darkness Maddy skied into a tree, tweaking his knee. So he did what any butt-burned, tweaked-knee backcountry wino would do: He took off his skis and started post-holing after his friend.

Greg, however, had his own problems. He lost the trail in the dark. After an hour the two decided to cut their losses and build a snow cave.

Once inside, they took their boots off, wrung the water from their socks, put their feet inside their packs and laid on top of one another to stay warm. But Lady Misfortune wasn't done. While Greg was on top of Maddy, the snow cave collapsed. "I was pinned inside under mounds of snow, with only my socks on," said Maddy. "And I was already hung over and had a fried butt."

By now the father of the bride had begun his toast, but none of us at Table 9 paid him any mind, leaning forward for the rest of Maddy's misfortune.

Greg, also in his socks, managed to slither out of the cave backwards and dig Maddy out. But the snow had buried their boots, and they couldn't them in the dark. So they made a lean-to in a nearby treewell and laid on each other once again, clenching and unclenching their shoeless, frostbitten toes. "We froze our asses off," said Maddy, "even though mine was burned. And we said Hail Mary's all night. We didn't bother with fictional stories of snuggling up to girls in a hot tub anymore."

At dawn, Greg found one of Maddy's boots and one of his and skied out for help, locating the trail a hundred yards away. Maddy, meanwhile, waited with his feet inside his backpack. Just as Greg arrived at the parking lot, a group of rescuers started off in snowmobiles to look for them, eventually loading up Maddy and sledding him to the parking lot where the media was eagerly waiting.

Paramedics gave them the once-over for frostbite and exposure, and then rushed them to the nearest hospital. "But no one knew about my butt," said Maddy. "They were just treating us for frostbite."

It wasn't until they were lying next to each other in their hospital beds that Greg leaned over and said, "Maddy, you have to tell them about your ass." Swallowing what was left of his pride, Maddy flagged down an assistant and told him his tale. "I leaned over from my bed and told this intern guy, 'Hey buddy, I didn't tell you guys everything. Something else happened up there. I kind of burned my butt.'"

Two minutes later the room was filled with nurses prodding and examining Maddy's rear. When they found out how it happened, they broke down in hysterics. "They were trying to be as professional as they could," continued Maddy, "but they couldn't help it."

Maddy spent the next two days with Greg, his female roommate and her sister. But it was a far cry from their fictional tales in the forest. "The funny thing," said Maddy, "is that he had a hot tub, but neither of us could use it…and that's after we had told all those hot tub fantasies on the trail."

Maddy ended the trip with a tweaked knee, frostbit feet, a burnt butt and an ego very much in check. The tough part, he said, wasn't that his eighth-grade students saw him on TV or that he missed two weeks of work, but that he couldn't walk—or sit down—for 14 days. "I had to stay off both my feet and my butt," he said. "I had to be on my stomach arched in front of the TV, or on an inner tube so my butt wouldn't touch anything." His roommate had it even worse; he had to peel the saturated gauze off Maddy's cheeks and change his bandages every day.

With that, Maddy leaned back in his chair and dabbed a napkin to his lips just as the father of the bride invited everyone to toast the newlyweds. Transfixed, none of us at Table 9 had any idea what we were toasting. Some wedding table conversations are just better than others.

Manly Men

"Nice robe."

The comment comes to John Allenberg from a stranger in the elevator at the Sutton Place in Revelstoke, B.C. It's hard not to acknowledge his bathwear. It's calf-length, jet-black fuzz, with a colorful, mountainous "Manly Men" logo embroidered on the breast. Similarly logoed hats and socks lie in his bedroom.

It's all swag for this year's annual Manly Men ski trip, of which I've somehow found myself involved. We've just ended day three of four, and so far it's lived up to its manly billing. Sandwiched around bell-to-bell skiing we've enjoyed bracketed ping-pong tournaments (they moved the penthouse suite's furniture to have a table delivered); over-priced, wine-filled dinners; beer-slamming happy hours; and, tonight, a weekend-ending Awards Party highlighting our transgressions.

Going on for nearly 50 years straight, the pilgrimage started at Grand Targhee in the early '70s by Joe Golden, whose wife lent it the testosterone term. Allenberg's dad was also an original, bringing him along in 1988 as it moved from Alta's Gold Miner's Daughter to the Alta Lodge. Allenberg has spearheaded it ever since, hence his nickname the Czar.

In its heyday, says Allenberg, an executive for apparel company Greensource, the trips peaked at about 30 guys, mostly family and friends from LA. In my inaugural inclusion, we're at 26 testicles, or 13.

General manliness is the only real caveat, as well as an affinity for partying and skiing. This year, after missing a flight from Vancouver, six of them hired a limo for an impromptu nine-hour drive to Rev, arriving trashed at 3 a.m. after break-dancing on the car floor for the last 100 miles. They were first in line that same morning.

It's the skiing that cements the brotherly bond. For the first three days, we posed for group photos, ripped top-to-bottom cruisers and sniffed out week-old powder stashes, returning each evening to après, hot tubs and full-course, glass-clinking meals.

Now it's our last night, with one more day of shredding before we leave. And as is often the case, the Manly Man above is looking out for his minions. It's shaping up to be a powder day, with huge flakes blanketing Revelstoke's 5,620 of vertical.

Changing from his black-fuzz bathrobe, the Czar later welcomes us in his penthouse suite for the awards dinner, where accolades are bestowed for Best Rookie, Best Injury and Best Partier. Three 10-person tables are set with black tablecloths. Cat the Masseuse and a cute blonde caterer are the only inklings of estrogen in the entire room. The Czar toasts everyone for attending the club's first venture across international borders. "Sometimes, our numbers have been big and sometimes they've dwindled, like salmon spawning upstream," he sways.

"Or like your sperm count," chides a manly listener.

And so it goes, the shit-giving as much a part of the weekend as the skiing. Later, another Manly Man projects a multi-media show onto the wall. The trip's antics come back to life amidst hoots and hollers, especially after a photo shows Allenberg passed out with a bottle cap balancing a ping pong ball on his forehead. Soon, it's time for us rookies to perform a mandatory talent show. Forfeiting our man cards, we borrow a skit I learned from my daughter's dance class whereby my buddy straddles my stomach and pretends he's a yoga instructor yanking at my legs. We're nearly bumping uglies, but it draws a chorus of manly laughs. Still, it's not enough to knock off international financier Shahan Soghikian from winning top greenhorn honors. This leads straight into the crown jewel ping pong tournament, complete with a manly March Madness bracket.

In the morning, the Manly Men are again first in line for the 15 inches blanketing the mountain. We shred it unsparingly until, one by one, we return home our separate ways to waiting wives and work. Our group sneaks in one last tree run down Conifers of Gnarnia before piling into our truck for the eight-hour drive back to Seattle, our quarters markedly tighter from our freshly sprouted chest hair.

Mom for the Holidays

She's gone. There, I said it. While we all have moms and other relatives who visit for the holidays, staying in tight quarters can often be taxing. Especially if your mom's a hair more eccentric than most.

It started when we arrived home at 6 p.m. Christmas Eve to find her car parked in our driveway and her sitting on the couch inside in pitch darkness.

"There you are...I couldn't find a light switch!" she exclaimed after I opened the front door and flipped on the switch, right where it's supposed to be.

We were more than happy to have her for a few days over the holidays. Then the bombshell hit. "Oh, I'm staying until Thursday!" she enthused, doubling her expected stay.

That's not to say we didn't welcome her or she didn't contribute. Among her food items: a half-full packet of wild rice that would feed two kindergarteners. My wife quickly noticed the expiration date of March 2010. "Rice doesn't expire," mom countered.

She controlled the pace of the next day's present-opening as much as she did foodstuffs. "Don't open that yet," she admonished our youngest as she reached for her stocking.

Her own presents came straight from the heart. I got a complete John McPhee collection of eight books, well-used with other people's markings in the margins. The highlight was a full-sized globe, which she ended up taking back to return for a cheaper model. It also led to an hour-long diatribe on Middle East history and policy.

The crux came when she gave our oldest daughter an ankle-length Buchanan Plaid skirt she made in the 1970s (a recipient since childhood of Buchanan Plaid boxers and scarves, I was thankfully spared). Forget that it's the ugliest tartan imaginable, a cacophony of yellow, greens and reds that matched our daughter's puke from Christmas Eve. The mothball smell trumped all. "You can't marry into plaid," my wife said, holding her nose to both odor and design.

On night three she made salad and French Onion soup—just the bellyful I craved after playing in a hockey tournament all day—washed down with a bottle of "expensive" wine. Ever the suspect, earlier my wife noticed that she had put a Zip-lock bag of moldy bacon in the fridge. As she took her last bite, she whispered, "Is this that bacon?" Sure enough, at the bottom of her bowl lay three small strips of the Grinch-colored flesh.

It was coincidence, of course, that our nine-year-old hurled her guts out two nights earlier on Christmas Eve, desecrating four comforters. But when my wife felt post-pork nausea, we connected the dots as if playing my daughter's Dollar Store stocking stuffer.

My mom, you see, has a garbage disposal for a stomach that's less, shall we say, discriminating than most other digestive systems. I came home for lunch one day, ate an apple and threw the core in the trash, and she fished it out, wiped the coffee grinds off and chomped in—all in front of my wide-mouthed daughter. Despite her intestinal toughness, she is allergic to cats, which might be why we have two—maybe next year our kids will find another one under the tree.

And like cats, at restaurants she feels a compelling need to lick everyone's plate clean before the server can collect them. "She's not done yet!" she exclaimed when our waiter tried to remove our daughter's plate, a lone pea wobbling near the rim. I could only slink in my chair hoping I didn't know our server. And even when she treats, you have to sneak back to add in more of a tip.

Toward the end of her stay she actually received an invitation from someone else of the elderly persuasion to go to gathering. But she missed the opportunity because she couldn't figure out how to answer our phone, fumbling with the TV remote instead.

While that might have gotten her out of our hair for a spell, she got back into it the final night when, in a moment of weakness, I agreed to let my 12-year-old play barber on me. It wouldn't have been so bad were it not for my mom swooping in like the cavalry. "Oh, I can fix it!" she exclaimed. Soon, both daughter and matriarch were doting around my head with scissors as I sat resigned to my follicled fate (notice no mugshot with this story?). "Looks a little longer on skier's left," said a friend shortly afterward.

On the bright side, she didn't get lost up on Emerald Mountain or slurp tomato juice off the counter like she has before, and she only forced us to watch one of her avant-garde DVDs. She might have micro-analyzed my investment portfolio, parked with her bumper overlapping our front step, and called a mem-stick of photos a joy-stick, but she also brought that same joy to our holidays. Which is why we look forward to her next visit, when, like that Motel 6 slogan, we'll make sure to leave the light on...

An Ode to Backcountry Bob

I only skied with him once, but the memory still lingers. It was at a "poachable" ski hut in Colorado's Never Summer Range, one he lived in for a month once after convincing backcountry rangers to let him stay.

Bob Casper held court the entire cramped night, partying like a rockstar—enough that he fell off the top bunk with a clap of thunder at 3 a.m.– and still leading the crack-of-dawn charge up and down No Name Peak the next morning. It's still one of the most aesthetic lines I've ever skied.

It's 22 years later and my buddy John McGowan, who spent two years skiing the backcountry of St. Anton with him, brings the memory back with bad news. "Did you hear Casper died?" he asks. "Committed suicide up in the Northwest."

John only found out about it because he hadn't heard from him for a spell—hence Bob's nickname "The Wind." "You wouldn't hear from him for a year, and then he'd show up on your doorstep, ready to roll out a huge adventure," he says. "Sometimes he'd stay for a month, driving wives crazy until he disappeared again." So John Googled him and discovered the bombshell.

"Anytime you skied with him you came away with an epic story," John reminisced, echoing my own Casper experience in Colorado. With that, he launched into a series of Casper tales, painting a picture of a skier who lived life by his own rules, and got others to do the same.

Exhibit A: He's Weber State, Utah's only full-ride, starting linebacker who would take solo, pre-dawn ski tours in the Wasatch before practice as extra training. With skiing options on our continent not big enough to contain him, from there Casper was Euro-bound, settling in St. Anton for eight years. While there, he became the region's most well-known off-piste skier—even the local "bergfuhrer" guides would tap the giant, wild-haired redhead for backcountry beta. "Fear just didn't exist for him," John waxes. "Whether skiing an improbable first descent with unthinkable consequences, or offending someone socially, he forged onward—consequences be damned."

He let his tracks—laid with his trusty Kastle 215 Super Gs and Salomon SX91 boots, with custom-mounted Vibram sole—speak for themselves, as long as an avalanche didn't wipe them out. His lore includes brazenly skiing the north face of Rendl above town, which hadn't been skied for 10 years ever since it slid and killed World Cup racing progeny Gertrude Gabl, the most talented skier in the valley. Casper's alpenglow-lit tracks straight down its gut remained there for days for all town to see.

Then there's the time he skied a couloir on the north face of Stuben only to have an avalanche carry him over a cliff and lawn-dart him between two shoulder-width boulders. Losing a trusty Kastle in the process, he skied out on one ski and hiked up the next summer to retrieve it. Or, when living in a basement flat in Haus Strolz in St. Jakob, he awoke to a massive avalanche filling his room up to the ceiling. While he escaped via a window above his bed, the kitchen cook above him, and six other townfolk, died.

"By all accounts, he shouldn't have walked away from that," John continues. "Bob wasn't looking for avalanches. Avalanches found Bob."

Another survival came when skiing Red Lady outside of Crested Butte, where he lived for 10 years after St. Anton. An avi ripped loose and carried him 300 yards, breaking his femur. Unburying himself, he one-leggedly post-holed as far as he could before building a snowcave—which collapsed in the middle of the night. The next morning he crawled out and waved down a passerby.

All this was all a result of a magnetic-like draw to aesthetic lines. "He had an uncanny ability for getting into trouble, and getting out of it," John espouses. "He was incredibly bold, which led to logging more pristine descents than most aspire to in many lifetimes."

But perhaps his greatest trait was getting others to traipse along. "He possessed a unique way of building intimate adventure alliances; of conveying that you'd been hand-picked as a co-conspirator to a serious ski descent," John says. "He'd single you out of a crowded pub at 2 a.m., whispering between clenched teeth with a ridiculous economy of words: 'You...me...Shindlergrat South Couloir...First Bahn.' The first time I heard it, I felt I had arrived in the coveted Casperian inner circle."

Social graces didn't come with the invitation. He wasn't much for them, be it talking smack on the football field, chatting-up strangers' girlfriends in a pub, or standing atop a cornice-lined peak. He lost his job as a bouncer at St. Anton's hottest club, the Hotel Alber, after stuffing the resort owner's father's face in the snow. He also had a propensity for taking a deuce at the top of every summit, for good luck. Once he did so atop France's Col du Chardonnet along the Haute Route, only to see a guide step in his pile a few minutes later in front of his clients. In trying to rub it off, the guide penetrated it deeper into his laces. "It had less to do with digestive function than some inner need to leave a physical monument to his ascent," says John. "You could depend on it religiously."

Alas, in the end it was his hand, rather than an avalanche's, that did him in. He took his life by gunshot at the Carbon River Entrance Station parking lot in Mount Rainier National Park on April 2, at age 49. His legacy is in how he led his life and encouraged others to do the same. "Ask anyone who knew him and they'd say that he was among the top influences in their life," says John, rattling off such lessons as passion, integrity, commitment and courage. "He taught us that there isn't a limit to energy expended in the pursuit of adventure; to grab life by the balls and not let go until it bends to your will; and that the only true risk in life is in trying to live life without risk."

While no one knows why such a talented skier so filled with life took his own, his final place of residence, as listed on his death certificate, seems only fitting: Black Diamond, Washington.

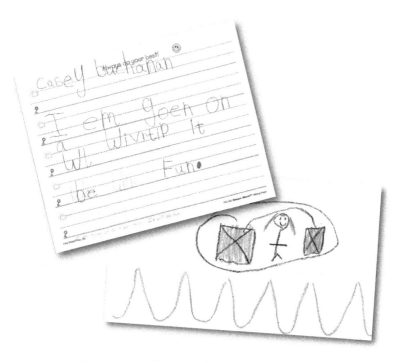

Recreating with Rugrats

I made it seven years in town before my recreational life—pressing glass on powder days, mountain biking at the drop of a helmet, and eddying out at Sunpies for a beer—changed forever. That's when my daughter, Brooke, was born and I became a...father in the 'Boat.

Not that it prompted a visit to Parents Anonymous ("Uh, my name is Eugene and I'm..."), but it did affect my happy-go-lucky approach to mountain town recreation. Gone were the days when I could rally on a moment's notice. Here, instead, was a new world of negotiating hall passes from my spouse, shorter play windows, and, more importantly, involving my kids in my outdoor pastimes.

Like climbing Mount Everest, the adjustment took some acclimating—whether armloading skis and poles onto the ski bus or quadrupling gear for any other outing. In the winter it meant surviving carrot and poma lift mishaps, skiing hunched over with back-tweaking kid leashes, and entering a new world of "secret passages" through the trees in Wally World.

Come spring, the melting snow exposed long-buried bike paths, playgrounds and parks, allowing the kids to play on ground again. (Yes, children, there's actual ground under that blanket of white.) As skis and sleds went into storage, out came the Trail-a-bikes, Burleys, pogo sticks and other gear. Getting creative, sometimes I'd even link the Burley behind the Trail-a-bike to create a triple-linked Dr. Seuss-mobile terrorizing the bike path, spelling wide turns and a grind up the hill home. I'd even huff it up to the Spring Creek ponds to fish for three-inch lunkers on Barbie rods, spending most of the time untangling lines. By August I'd know which parks had the longest slides, highest swings and most inconvenient bathrooms.

I'd also cram the kids into an inflatable kayak, stopping for mid-calf soaks at the Rich Weiss Park hot springs and cannonballing into the C- and D-holes downtown. Social Services notwithstanding, once I even caged my youngest Casey in her pack-n'-play crib on shore while I swam with Brooke. When they were older, we'd search for the secret rock "Latch" in the D-hole, letting us dolphin against the current.

We'd hike to Gold Creek Lake—or as far as the kids would let us—throwing sticks and playing Hide and Seek to keep them going, with the lure of Clark Store ice cream cones afterward. We'd rock climb Blob Rock, Casey pendulumming like a piñata while getting lowered in her harness. And we'd barbecue at Elk Park, letting the swing play babysitter while the grown-ups tossed horseshoes.

Of course, as they got older we got sucked into the more time-consuming and conventional pastimes of other urban parents—coaching soccer ("Stop blowing those dandelions and get over here!"), fetching balls on the tennis courts ("Nice home run!") and embarking on cross-town shuttle-athons to gymnastics, dance and swim lessons. I even picked them up from soccer practice at Emerald Fields in a raft once.

Throughout all this I learned that, like the Grinch trying to stop Christmas, having kids in a mountain town doesn't end your recreational pleasures at all. It just changes. To borrow a climbing term, you can still feed your own rat; you just include the rugrats as well..

Skating Over Skiing

Okay, okay, so I missed the biggest powder dump of the year. Go ahead and rub it in. But the rest of you didn't get to watch 12-year-old girls play hockey in the state playoffs.

That's right, last weekend marked the state playoffs for the U-12, -14 and -19 girls hockey teams at Denver's Edge Ice Arena. So while the rest of you were getting face shots, us proud parents of pucksters were watching face-offs and slap shots.

The weekend capped a winter of home games and throw-up-filled road trips, culminating with a berth in the finals, held serendipitously every year on the last weekend of Blues Break. It's a rite of passage for players and parents alike, each growing from the experience. It's where a year's worth of stick taping, lace tying, helmet buckling, elbow pad re-fastening and more lace tying and tear drying all comes to a head in four final games.

While the girls learn valuable sportsmanship, teamsmanship and other ship skills, so too do the parents. We're thrown into new social circles, polishing up tactics to remember other parents' names; we hone anger management skills, keeping cool in face of botched calls; we mnemonically contrive ways to match kids' names with their jersey numbers; and we become masters of the shared shuttle, packing kids and gargantuan gear bags into every ounce of car space, more for saving sanity than fossil fuels.

The payoff is witnessing moments you'll remember far longer than any powder day: the huddling up singing "We will rock you!" before game time; the laying on bellies in a giant star around the goalie before the starting buzzer; the hugs, high fives and fist-bumps after someone scores, even if the game's already out of reach; and the embracing of the goalie after the final whistle, even if it wasn't exactly a shut-out.

Throughout it all, we take our place in the stands next to other like-minded parents from places like Vail, Aspen and Crested Butte, whom all look like they're from those towns. An Aspen mom cuddles a white poodle; the Crested Butte crowd is more grizzled and facial-haired than the rest; and the Vail fans cheer like they're at the World Cup.

Collectively, we "oooh!" and "aaaah!" every shot and save; will pucks to veer toward the goal; second-guess penalties like we're Barry Melrose minus the mullet; and raise our eyebrows at the overly enthusiastic (do you really need to stand up and cheer for that ninth goal when you're up 8-0?).

Meanwhile, the kids play on, oblivious to the parental drama above. They're Energizer Bunnies, some playing seven games in 40 hours, with any available rest time taken up playing laser tag. It's a juggling act of feeding, shuttling, dressing and playing that would do any military commander proud.

The logistics continue at the hotel lobby, where a giant pizza, Pad Thai and adult beverage potluck scares all other guests back into their rooms. Like line changes on the ice, the socializing comes in waves, parents from different age groups arriving with the timing of their games. The overlap supercharges the mingling, a veritable Steamboat on C-470.

Once fed, the kids come and go between games of elevator tag, Jacuzzi dips, dance contests and forays outside. You wonder how they're even standing when curfew comes and they head to bed, only to wake at 6 a.m. to do it all again.

When the weekend's over—after you watch them win a lone game and dogpile the goalie; after they celebrate in the locker room like they won the Stanley Cup; and after you give in and buy that "must have" team photo—you pack up and return home, driving through the same storm that saved the ski season like a goalie glove.

But you don't care. So you missed the season's biggest snowfall. There'll be more. Your daughter's comment seals it: "That was fun," she sums up in the car, her smile already cementing next Blues Break's plans.

Welcome to Gamberville

It's 6 a.m. on a Wednesday morning on a 2,000-vertical-foot catwalk leading to Thunderhead Lodge at the top of the gondola. Before the groomed corduroy ridges have a chance to reflect the early morning light, a lone figure scars their parallel lines with diagonal Vs. While most locals are still snug in bed, Big Agnes owner Bill Gamber already has his day's activity in.

Not that he won't try to fit in another. If it's a powder day, he'll be back out. Or maybe he'll coach his sons Max, Bennett, and now Fritz in their cross country program that afternoon. Or maybe he'll bike to his house atop a dirt road six miles out of town and don skins to lay a few tracks out his front door.

Then there's his competitive side. He holds the 12-hour solo record for the local 24 Hours of Steamboat mountain bike race (112 miles, 20,000 vertical feet), and has competed in more than 100 triathlons, including 16 Ironmans. His top finish was taking 50th in the Canadian Ironman, out of a field of 2,000. Not bad for someone who juggles a family and three successful companies with the same aplomb he does triathlons' disciplines.

For Gamber, it's all in a day's work ... literally. And he approaches his companies—fleece apparel-maker BAP!, energy food company Honey Stinger, and tent and sleeping bag manufacturer Big Agnes—with the same passion he brings to his sporting pursuits.

"My personality definitely fits with working hard," he says from his what-used-to-be-cramped office downtown, The Clash's "London Calling" blaring in the background and Susan Snyder's book, Past Tents, laying haphazardly on a nearby bookshelf. "I'm about as committed running my businesses as I am competing in triathlons."

That's a scary thought, and one that lies at the core of Big Agnes' success. He emails his Chinese manufacturers from home after the kids are in bed, and can be seen in his office before the local coffee shops are open (not that he drinks it, an even scarier thought). After a recreation binge resulted in knee surgery, he once worked a tradeshow booth with an IV still attached to his arm.

"He definitely brings the same intensity from his rec life to the work place," admits partner Rich Hager, who splits duties with third owner Len Zanni. "When competing, he never used to have anything on the line other than his ego. Now he has that, plus his family, house and livelihood."

Gamber picked up all three after moving to Steamboat in 1990. He had already started BAP! in college at Loch Haven, Pennsylvania, selling bike shorts to fund his triathlon habit, and worked construction and guided rock climbing while getting BAP! off the ground. "My business hobby supported my triathlon hobby," he says of his unorthodox beginnings.

Borrowing a name from the nearby Mount Zirkel Wilderness Area—a theme that runs through its entire line—Big Agnes was born in 2001 with a simple line of innovative sleeping bags whose pad slides into a sleeve, reducing material and weight. Inc. magazine thought the concept interesting enough that it profiled the company its first year, but it didn't pull any punches. "A lot of people didn't think we would make it," says Gamber. "They thought the market was too crowded. But we saw it as an opportunity because there wasn't much innovation."

That innovation didn't happen overnight—especially the cold November evening he and Hager tested the first prototype after a three-hour night-skin from his house. After building a snow cave and crawling into their product, sweet dreams turned soggy when the cave collapsed and the pad and bag weren't exactly a seamless fit. "It was back to the drawing board after that," says Hager. "But then we got the kinks worked out."

Whatever they did worked, with REI jumping on board as a retailer the first year. Two years later Big Agnes rolled out its first tents, the Seedhouse and Mad House, also to rave reviews. From three bags and six pads in year one to today's complement of 52 bags, five liners, 10 pads, 28 tents, seven tarps and shelters, as well as luggage, drybags, pillows, hammocks and more, business continues to nearly double every year.

And at every product's root is a basic human essential. "We started by just trying to create a more comfortable sleeping system," says

Gamber. "Somehow we managed to bridge the gap between comfort and high performance."

Now they've bridged the gap between small upstart and major player, with REI going from their first arm-twisting buy of pads and bags in year one to carrying multiple products in all stores. "They've done really well in innovation," says REI Product Manager Tom Kimmet. "They're able to see a trend and act on it very quickly."

Case in point: Kimmet cites a year when two-man tent sales remained flat and three-mans jumped 28 percent. That same year, Big Agnes rolled out its three-person Emerald Mountain, filling a niche before anyone even knew it was needed. Kimmet credits this industry foresight to Gamber. "He has great partners, but the company exists on the sheer will of Bill," he says. "He has a great vision of what needs to happen next, is willing to take risks and is eager to launch new products. He always has something in his back pocket that he wants to show you—there's a little bit of mad scientist to him."

Case in point number two: In 2017 Big Agnes debuted the AXL and Insulated AXL sleeping pads, weighing 9 and 10 ounces respectively, the lightest in the category.

This analogy carries through to company number two. Two years after founding Big Agnes, Gamber launched Honey Stinger, which specializes in honey-based bars, gels, chews and waffles. Though his family has been in the honey business for more than 60 years (his grandfather designed the plastic honey bear), he came up with the brainstorm to add electrolytes and flavorings. That company, too, is benefiting from Gamber's golden-as-honey touch, with sales increasing annually.

But it's Big Agnes that keeps him busier than a Honey Stinger bee, and that contributes the most margin to the bottom line. And it's this bee-like work ethic that keeps the accolades coming, including countless Editor's Choice awards from national magazines.

Just as in his triathlon training, Gamber instills performance as the bottom line. He drills this into his 100 employees between Big Agnes and Honey Stinger (and 30 external sales reps), who split time between a new 20,500-square-foot office and 8,000-square-foot warehouse.

Just as important is his business acumen, keeping a keen eye on supplier and manufacturing costs. "There aren't that many independent outdoor companies that have grown as much as Big Agnes has," says Kimmet. "For them to do that as an independent is a testament to their operation."

His biggest challenge now is managing his company's growth while continuing its trademark innovation. He's also taking his company green. All pads and bags containing PrimaLoft are now be made of PrimaLoft Eco, made from 50 percent recycled bottles. Others are made from 100 percent recycled insulation and 100 percent recycled fabric.

How does he fit it all in, juggling three businesses with a three-child family and a recreation life that would do a trustfunder proud? For one, he sets his watch 10 minutes fast. But more importantly, he loves what he does and where he does it. "I don't think you can be very good at something that you don't like to do," he says. "We're authentic—if we want to test a tent, we do it right here in our backyard."

Just like balancing a triathlon's disciplines, he often combines family, business and recreation into one. He'll camp at Hahn's Peak Lake for four days with his kids, testing product (and his wife's patience) at night, while biking 70 miles roundtrip each day to work in Steamboat. Another time, he got busted for speeding after leaving his house at midnight to night climb and ski Sleeping Giant mountain before flying out to China at 6:30 a.m. He was wearing his tele boots when the cop pulled him over. Or the time he squeezed in a ski descent of iconic Silver Couloir outside Silverthorne en route to flying out of DIA for a meeting with REI that afternoon in Seattle, with nary a rub of deodorant. Or "product testing" in the Mount Zirkel Wilderness Area for three days with staff, returning just as the first Powerpoint slide began for a company-hosted presentation by the Colorado Water Trust, burrs still embedded in his Smartwools.

The only downside to his breakneck pace is that his family often has to keep up; when his nephews once visited, one left with a broken collarbone and another with a concussion.

But he's not likely to slow down, with more market share waiting. "It's funny," he says. "I wasn't very competitive when I started racing triathlons, either. But you just put your head down and stick with it and good things seem to happen. "

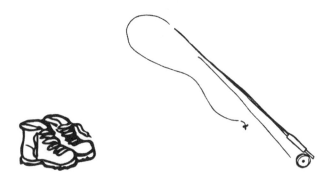

Special Thanks to the following Tales from a Mountain Town Sponsors!

202

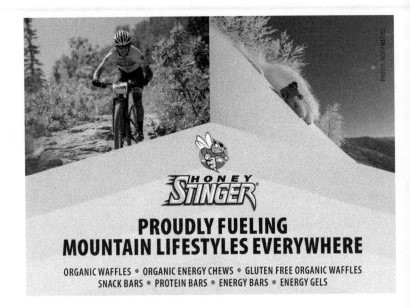

No Better Feeling.

There are never enough hours in the day. That's why we create warm, breathable layers that help you make the most of every minute. Because when the temperature drops and everyone else has called it a day, we're still ready for more.

About The Author

A former reporter for the *Denver Business Journal* and 14-year editor-in-chief of *Paddler* magazine, Eugene Buchanan has written about the outdoors for more than 25 years, from covering the X Games for ESPN.com to working for NBC at the Beijing Olympics. An avid adventurer with articles published in the *New York Times, Men's Journal, Sports Afield, Outside, National Geographic Adventure* and more, he's a member of New York's prestigious Explorer's Club and the founder of www.paddlinglife.net. He's the author of Brothers on the Bashkaus; Outdoor Parents, Outdoor Kids (a winner of the Living Now Book Awards); and Comrades on the Colca. He lives with his wife, Denise, and daughters, Casey and Brooke, in Steamboat Springs, Colorado.

Order at www.eugenebuchanan.com

CPSIA information can be obtained
at www.ICGtesting.com
Printed in the USA
FSHW04n1457200318
45733FS

9 780692 992128